FACES OF A RESERVATION

FACES OF A

RESERVATION

A Portrait of the Warm Springs Indian Reservation

Text and Photographs by

CYNTHIA D. STOWELL

☐ OREGON HISTORICAL SOCIETY PRESS ☐

Cover: *Mary Hote / A view of the land of the Warm Springs Indian Reservation / Robert Macy, Sr.*

Frontis: *Bumper stickers on a Warm Springs car proclaim pride in all three of the reservation's tribes. (Cynthia D. Stowell)*

Library of Congress Cataloging-Publication Data

Stowell, Cynthia D., 1951-
  Faces of a reservation.
  Bibliography: p.
  Includes index.
  1. Warm Springs Indian Reservation (Or.)   2. Indians of North America—Oregon—History.   3. Indians of North America—Oregon—Biography.   I. Title.
E78.06S86 1987 979.5'62 86—31263
ISBN 0-87595-190-2
ISBN 0-87595-203-8 (paperback)

Second printing 1989

Printed in the United States of America.

"Commerce, even back in the early days, was an important part of our people's lifestyle. The arena of commerce may have changed, but the concept of helping to sustain ourselves has not. Through continuous economic development and prudent use of our resources, we hope to provide for the better livelihood of our members. This can be the legacy for our generation and generations yet unborn."

Tribal administrator ☐
at dedication of
hydro-electric power project

"We're a pitiful people, we're a lost people. We're searching for this and searching for that and leaning against each other. We're forgetting our culture."

Tribal elder ☐
at a general council meeting

CONTENTS

viii

FACES OF A RESERVATION

FOREWORD

FOR THOUSANDS OF YEARS, the ancestors of the people of Warm Springs lived comfortably in "Middle Oregon." A moderate climate, an abundance of nutritious plants, and plentiful fish and game made their lives comparatively easy. Perhaps as a result of living in a land of plenty, they developed the characteristics displayed to the first white settlers. They welcomed non-Indians just as they had welcomed other Indian tribes to visit their land. They were generous, friendly, and accommodating. ☐ The Indians historically had roamed freely through the ten million acres of central Oregon hunting, fishing, digging roots, gathering berries, and changing village locations. The white man returned the hospitality by insisting on private ownership of "his" land and by restricting the movement of the Indians. By the Treaty of 1855 the United States demanded that the tribes be located on a reservation with the announced view of protecting the Indians from the whites. The real purpose was to make Indian land available to settlers. The tribes ceded ten million acres of central Oregon and reserved only about 540,000 of those same acres for their own use. Because their entire culture was based on fishing and hunting, they also reserved their right to fish, hunt, and gather foods in their usual and accustomed places off the reservation. But the die was cast. The people of Warm Springs were moving a giant step away from their traditions and a way of life that had been with them for thousands of years. Many more steps had to be taken. While those have been difficult steps, what was a hopeless situation for the Warm Springs Tribes in 1855 may now be one of great hope. ☐ More than one hundred thirty years since the treaty was signed, Cynthia Stowell demonstrates a re-

markable understanding of the Tribes' suffering and their struggles against almost hopeless odds.

Life was difficult on the reservation. By a supplemental, fraudulent treaty of 1865, an attempt was made to eliminate what was most important to them —their off-reservation fishing and hunting rights. It took 104 years before United States District Judge Robert Belloni put an end to that infamous document. In 1871 an "erroneous" survey took 61,000 acres off the north and west lines of the reservation. Not until 100 years later was that corrected by the Congress.

They were told to be farmers. What a cruel hoax! When the treaty was signed, government agents reported to Congress that the land was mountainous, rocky, had poor soil, and was covered with timber so that it was unlikely the white settlers would ever wish to occupy it.

The Dawes Severalty (Allotment) Act of 1887 proved to be the undoing of many reservations throughout the country. The Congress, with good intentions, legislated for the division of Indian reservations into small acreages that were to be allotted to individual Indians. The allotments could then be converted to fee patent status making it available for non-Indian ownership. Fortunately, before the Warm Springs Reservation was totally destroyed, the Indian Reorganization (Wheeler-Howard) Act of 1934 stopped the allotments and permitted Indian tribes to organize. The Wheeler-Howard Act finally gave Indians limited control over their own destiny.

With that the people of Warm Springs made a wise decision. They elected to incorporate under the Act and to begin to manage their lives and their property. By the early 1950s, they made the decision to become economically independent. They wisely concluded this was the only way to avoid the "Termination Fever" that was guiding the Congress on a path to eliminate Indian tribes and Indian reservations.

Wise decisions in the management of timber, beneficial contracts with Portland General Electric on the Pelton and Round Butte dams, and a determination to succeed and survive began to have an impact. The economy improved and then boomed.

The Tribes acquired a sawmill and a plywood plant.

They bought back their historic hot springs property on the Warm Springs River, which had fallen into private ownership as a result of the Allotment Act, and developed Kah-Nee-Ta Resort. The special legislation that authorized this repurchase and returned it to trust or reservation status also permitted the reacquisition of other lands that had gone into fee patent status as a result of the Allotment Act. The checkerboarding that occurred with the Allotment Act was being eliminated at Warm Springs. The Tribes built the new Kah-Nee-Ta Lodge, reacquired the 61,000 acres in the McQuinn Strip, started an innovative housing program, and constructed new community facilities throughout the reservation. Electricity was extended to the rural areas and there was a new confidence at Warm Springs. It was really becoming a "distinct political community" as Indian tribes were defined by Chief Justice John Marshall in the celebrated case of *Worcester* v. *Georgia* in 1832.

As the tribal attorney for twenty-five years, I participated in some of these historic events, sharing both disappointments and victories with the people. *Faces of a Reservation* lets the reader witness more than a century of such suffering and happiness. Further, Ms. Stowell's words and photographs invite vicarious participation in the wonderful festivals and celebrations and in the impressive funeral traditions that give a special rhythm to life at Warm Springs. In these pages, we experience an all-night wake in the longhouse with singing, dancing, testimony, and tears. There is the excitement of the Washat or Seven Drum religious services and the "white noise" of the Shaker Church. There is the newer tradition of the Presbyterian Church founded in 1874 and the blending of Christian and native religions. There are the powwows, the rodeos, the feasts, and the day-to-day pursuits of a community determined to survive. People have studied and lived a lifetime with the Indians to gain the perspective that Ms. Stowell conveys in such a beautiful and interesting way.

Hon. Owen M. Panner
Chief Judge, U.S. District Court
Portland, Oregon

ACKNOWLEDGEMENTS

A S THE PIECES OF this book fell into place and I began to realize that my work soon would be bound between two covers, certain names and faces came flooding naturally into my mind. They belong to the people who, either consciously or inadvertently, helped this project see the light of day. First a few personal messages. To Emily and Jim Åkerson, Alice and Jimmy Florendo, Nancy and Clay Garrison, Faye Waheneka and family, Bernice and Art Mitchell, and Kenman and Sue: I greatly appreciate the shelter you gave me in Warm Springs after I'd pulled up my own stakes. To the folks at *Spilyay Tymoo*: Thanks for the use of your office as a pit stop and work space, and for free access to the negative files. To Richard Macy: Your standard greeting "Is your book done yet?" helped keep me going. ☐ And to friends and family who believed in my work or at least decided to humor me until I either gave up or finished, I hope the book is worth all my one-sentence Christmas cards, non-existent letters and phone calls, and redundant progress reports. Clarence, thanks for being there and not being there at just the right times. ☐ My professional gratitude goes to: Owen Panner for his review of the manuscript, his enthusiastic support, and his contribution of the Foreword; Kathrine French, for her very thorough eleventh-hour reading and her generous gift of time and knowledge (with behind-the-scenes help from David French); Larry Calica, for his "light reading" and sensitive suggestions; Charles Wilkinson for eyeballing an early draft and offering some spontaneous insights; Hank Morrison, for reading and reacting to drafts of my introduction and for answering linguistics questions; the Confederated Tribes, first for employing me, and then for not only tolerating

my project but also providing facts, figures, and impressions and trusting me to use them wisely; and Portland State University, for letting me reduce my appointment to finish up the book, and for maintaining a fine periodicals collection. Special appreciation goes to my editors at the Press, Bruce Hamilton (who had a hunch about this project from the start) and Adair Law (who came into the project late but with a deft red pen), and to the Oregon Historical Society for recognizing that history is what is happening today and for preserving it in its handsome publications.

Thanks to the following for permission to reproduce illustrations that they control: Confederated Tribes of Warm Springs; Dan Macy; National Archives; Oregon Historical Society; Smithsonian Institution; *Spilyay Tymoo*; and the University of Oregon Library. Thanks also to Elizabeth Woody for contributing the poem about her grandmother.

It is almost impossible to properly acknowledge the people whose faces fill this book. All I can say is that you feel like a big family to me, and I'll try to be a good granddaughter, daughter, sister, and cousin despite the miles that come between us and the years that go by.

A NOTE FROM THE FIFTY-THIRD FACE

THERE IS ONE FACE that does not show up in these pages, though its presence is felt in every word and picture. How it happens to keep hidden company with the fifty-two faces in this volume is worth some explanation. ☐ Warm Springs was my home for almost seven years. There clearly had been others from Boston before me—the Wasco word for white man is *bushtn*. But soon after arriving in 1975, I learned that bushtns do not simply decide to live on an Indian reservation unless they have friends or a job. I had neither—just a vague notion of a photo essay about Northwest tribes and enough money to last six months to a year. It was pure luck that Alice's Restaurant accepted raw recruits as waitresses. ☐ Alice was a kind of self-appointed gatekeeper. "If you can get past me, you can get along with anybody on the reservation," she told me, a statement that leaps to mind when we are having our differences twelve years later. Suspicious of my motivations, Alice nevertheless tried to orient me to the community, stage whispering from the kitchen, "That's a chief!" or "That man is our general manager!" or "Hurry up with that soup! He's high up in the tribal administration!" ☐ Before I had learned to balance plates on my arms, I was off on the trail of the new tribal newspaper. But when I took my small portfolio to a non-Indian administrator, he practically escorted me to the next bus out of town, saying rather protectively, "They don't like anthropologists around here, you know." Warm Springs Elementary, on the other hand, welcomed my camera and notebook and asked me to work with a group of sixth graders on assembling a word and picture portrait of the reservation. Alice didn't lose much of a waitress.

That same spring, Coyote loped into my life. Sid Miller, the editor selected to guide the new *Spilyay Tymoo* (Coyote News), called and said he needed some help in the darkroom. By the third issue, I was shooting, writing, and learning lay-out. Little else mattered for the next three years.

It took some time for the community and its first newspaper—with its two bushtn reporters—to feel comfortable together. But soon, a reporter's presence was expected—at times demanded—at all but sacred gatherings. With hardly an evening or weekend to myself, I became completely wrapped up in the workings of the Confederated Tribes, developing a fierce loyalty as well as an insider's critical eye. After a long day at-large in the community—from budget meetings to cattle rides—it was often a shock to come home to my trailer, look in the mirror, and see a white face.

I left *Spilyay* after three-and-a-half years, fatigued and ready to meet the community on new terms. I was only sketchily aware of the reservation world beyond the administration building and public events, and I wanted to know the individuals who inhabited it—the people behind the Tribes' three-tepee logo.

Taking on just enough free-lance work to make ends meet, I began to spend more time in people's homes, just sitting and visiting. I joined in private religious ceremonies, stopped in at taverns, and followed people to work. And I listened. I listened to hopes and frustrations, diatribes and meanderings, voices of the ambitious and productive, of the lonely and confused. The voices confirmed what I had begun to believe—that there is no single truth about the Warm Springs Reservation. There is a collective identity based on ethnicity, history, and cultural tradition, a unified otherness built on adversity, and a carefully constructed public image created by tribal leaders. But beneath the surface, there are as many faces to Warm Springs as there are tribal members. And there are as many ways to experience Warm Springs as there are visitors to it, depending on where they come from, why they are there, and who they know. At last I had a direction for the book that I had been dreaming about. I would profile individuals whose thoughts and lives together shape the community I had come to know.

The people in this collection were hand-picked in an absolutely unscientific manner. They are friends, acquaintances, people I always wanted to know but wasn't sure how to approach, prominent figures, or individuals I sought out because they had a particular occupation or opinion that I felt should be represented. Despite the varying relationships I've had with these people, the terms by which we worked together were the same. Every photographic and written portrait in this book appears with the review and permission of the participant. Sometimes this was achieved with one conversation, one shooting, and one writing, and other times it took months of pursuing, negotiating, rewriting, and reshooting.

It was a collaborative effort that admittedly invited compromise, but it seemed to be the fairest way to treat a community that has suffered repeatedly from curious and exploitive visitors. The reservation as a whole has a passion for privacy, and while individuals tend to be remarkably open when talking about their personal lives, they are careful about what they reveal publicly. "*You* can say whatever you want, but *I* have to live here the rest of my life," is a common refrain. There were some telling details and ironic twists that had to be sacrificed because people simply could not live with them. There also were some heart-breaking withdrawals from participation: one woman who had allowed me to photograph and write about her husband's funeral came to believe that this break in tradition had aggravated her and her family's grieving process, and I respectfully shelved the material; a young friend whose potential was continually thwarted by bad luck felt I had missed the point of his first twenty-five years, and he bowed out. Some friendships were strained during the course of my chronicling; some relationships never got off the ground. But in more cases than not, warm and rewarding associations developed out of the intense mutual work.

Then there was the matter of Warm Springs politeness. It is unsettling to wonder how many people gave their approval not out of any real comfort with what I had written but out of the Warm Springs tendency to appear cooperative. If this book had a formal dedication, it would be to these gentle persons, as well

as to those more forceful folks who weren't afraid to say "no."

I've come to realize that if a Warm Springer had taken on this project, it would have turned out quite differently. For the people who live there, the Warm Springs Reservation is one living organism, with tribes and families—not individuals—as the principal functioning parts. Singling out individuals for special recognition flies in the face of Warm Springs propriety.

But, far from invalidating my book, these several disclaimers only serve to illustrate the lively, sometimes perplexing, dynamics that characterize the meeting of two cultures. I can't count the number of times I've heard people in Warm Springs say, as if by rote, "Only an Indian can understand how an Indian thinks and feels." At first, in my liberal open-mindedness and empathy, I objected. But after a dozen years, I can see a profound truth in those seemingly ethnocentric words. At times I have talked like an Indian, behaved like an Indian, identified with Indians, and felt more comfortable with Indians than with whites. I can intellectually understand, I can empathize, I can have moments of great insight. I can even say, after years as a minority in an otherwise homogeneous community, that I know what it feels like to be judged by skin color and to be politically powerless. But can I ever truly experience the feeling of having roots entwined with hundreds of other people in a piece of ground that is at once native and alien, in a culture that reaches back through millennia? Probably not.

This conclusion need not be discouraging. It does not imply perpetual misunderstandings and conflict between cultures. Rather, it is exciting to acknowledge those differences and to reach as far as we can into another's camp without disturbing the natural order around the hearth and without forgetting our own origins. Ideally, we come back from such forays with enhanced sensitivity and the desire to have others understand what we've learned.

Part of me will never come back, I know that. I've left behind in Warm Springs a measure of innocence, some ideological baggage, and a corner of my heart. But I've brought along a few familiar faces so that others might know them, too. I've woven their stories together with mine to help reveal a kind of fragile truth about the reservation. It is the truth about one extended encounter with a community—about the many small encounters with suspicion, politeness, respect, trust, and intimacy that characterize the delicate process of people getting to know one another. This book is my gift to the people of Warm Springs. And it is their gift to me.

INTRODUCTION

WARM SPRINGS, OREGON. A rural community on the road to somewhere else. Much like the next place, it has hamburgers, gasoline, and rest rooms for the traveler. Stay awhile and there are fireworks on the Fourth of July, and Little League in the evenings, bake sales at noon, rodeos on the weekends, and revivals whenever spirits are moved. Gossip abounds and newcomers are eyed warily. Change comes too quickly for some, too slowly for others. ☐ Warm Springs Indian Reservation. In this place, far from the American heartland, people can hear the voices of their ancestors echoing from the basalt-rimmed canyon walls, telling them in an ancient language when to gather the earth's foods and what songs to sing in the longhouse, what to name their children, and how to grieve for the dead. Here, within boundaries drawn by the federal government more than a century ago, the people strive for continuity with their own separate past. ☐ Warm Springs flirts with the familiar, giving a nod to the uniformity of twentieth century American life, but then it dances away, delighting in its differentness. Demanding and defending it. Occasionally despairing over it. A finely tuned tension exists between Warm Springs and the rest of the world. ☐ It goes back to the way in which the gentle valley of Warm Springs was first settled, and even farther back to another homeland and another way of life. The Warm Springs people's ancestors along the Columbia River and in the Great Basin did not choose this new home. While towns were being founded all over the Oregon Territory by idealistic farmers, loggers, ranchers, and miners, the federal government created the Warm Springs Indian Reservation as a repository for people who were in the way of

frontier progress. The three tribes who came to live here had their own names for themselves and for the rivers, springs, and promontories they had known from a distance, but when the Treaty of 1855 reserved this acreage on the east slopes of the Cascade Mountains, new names were needed. The people came to be called "The Confederated Tribes" and the place, "The Warm Springs Reservation of Oregon."

The reservation was chosen as a solution to the "Indian problem" in many more places than Oregon. During the nineteenth century, treaties and executive orders created nearly one hundred and fifty reservations across the United States, six of them in Oregon. Also established was a huge federal bureaucracy designed to protect the reservation land held in trust for the tribes, to make reservation policy, and to deliver services to reservation Indians.

It is not surprising that the people of Warm Springs can often identify more easily with an Indian reservation two thousand miles away than with their white neighbors across the Deschutes River. Decades of federal supervision characterized by one generation of bureaucrats, congressmen, judges, or social reformers unilaterally trying to correct the mistakes of the previous generation have amalgamated Indian tribes into a strong political, social, and spiritual community.

This was not always so. At the time of European contact, the diverse native peoples of North America had little but the continent in common, at least from their viewpoints. Despite many of the tribes' own genesis myths, anthropologists maintain that today's North and South American Indians are descendants of hunters and gatherers who migrated from Asia during the last Ice Age. Biologists view Indians as a genetic group with a particular distribution of blood types, a characteristic facial structure, and a common hair color and texture that link them with the people of Eastern Asia. But the native groups always saw themselves as quite distinct from one another, as evidenced by the many traditional tribal names that translate into English as "the People." Cultural insensitivity and political expediency on the part of white newcomers lumped all the "People" into one group known erroneously as

Indians, after Columbus' discovery of what he thought was the East Indies. Subsequent federal policy has given little consideration to tribal and cultural differences, since the government's aim was not to preserve native cultures but to isolate them and then to methodically assimilate the natives themselves into the mainstream of American culture.

Indians did seem to be vanishing for a time. Those who survived the devastation of European diseases and the inroads of the U.S. Army were faced with isolation and deprivation on the new reservations. Without familiar means of providing for themselves and no voice in planning their futures, reservation populations declined in numbers and in spirit. Countless individuals left the reservations in pursuit of job opportunities, often as part of government relocation programs, only to disappear into urban wilderness. Until the Red Power movement of the 1960s, many Indians actually hid their racial and cultural identity, having internalized the distaste shown for them by generations of government teachers and administrators.

Yet Indians did not disappear and neither did the reservations. Although today only about half the nation's 1.3 million Indians live on reservations, these tribal land bases and the treaties that created them are the nucleus for "Indian country," a tangible reminder that Indian tribes have certain aboriginal and treaty rights and that the government therefore has special responsibilities to Indian tribes.

An Indian woman from Oregon said to me, after hearing about my book, "You should call it 'Faces of *the Warm Springs* Reservation.'" I knew what she was getting at. No two reservations are the same, and to single out one as representative could be misleading, if not downright disrespectful of tribal differences. And yet, to ignore the common themes running through the reservation experience would be to dismiss several hundred years of American history and to write off Warm Springs as an anachronism. To be sure, there is no other place on earth like Warm Springs, but anyone who has lived on an Indian reservation will feel at least a little bit at home here.

Like many reservations, it is a home in the fullest

sense of the word. Never mind the typically high unemployment, short life spans, chronic alcoholism, teenage pregnancies, and high pupil drop-out rates. The reservation is a comfortable haven from an alien world, the preferred place to live for most who are born there. On the "outside," where life is busy, impersonal, and driven by the clock and calendar, individuals are left to sink or swim on their own. On the reservation, faces are familiar, services are easy to find and often free, people will laugh at your jokes or understand your despair, and relatives are all around. It can be a cruel place, too. The quarters are close and the memories are long, with tribal or family feuds passed along from generation to generation. But when it comes time to resist an encroachment from the outside, to celebrate, or to mourn, those rifts can close up and form very solid ground.

And there is the land itself. It may not be the people's ancestral home, but generations have lived there and come to love its contours and its smells. Whether or not it has economic potential, that land is one constancy for a people weary of change, a political foundation on which they can build their futures.

In a nation where the ownership of land and the development of natural resources are sources of power and influence, landed Indian tribes have a head start over their urban counterparts. Much to the dismay of those bureaucrats who saw reservations as mere stepping-stones to assimilation, reservation Indians are just starting to settle in. Taking what they have collectively learned from their long exposure to Anglo law and commerce, they are beginning to pump life into their reservation governments and economies as a way to ensure their survival as distinct peoples.

The Warm Springs Reservation has taken this strategy to heart. Blessed with rich natural resources and careful leaders, Warm Springs has made strides toward self-sufficiency that other reservations have only dreamed about. In its diversity of enterprises and its relative prosperity, it is a showpiece reservation, respected in both Indian and white circles. When steeped in this success story, it is easy to forget that Warm Springs is unusual among reservations, that there is more hope here than almost anywhere else in "Indian country." While many other reservations have a great deal more acreage, they lack the natural advantages—the resources, the location, the beauty—that Warm Springs enjoys.

This is the face that the Confederated Tribes of the Warm Springs Reservation most wants the general public to see: the sophisticated tribal corporation providing for its "shareholders" in an atmosphere of growth and optimism. It is the face the media currently want to focus on, too; "Indian capitalists" have supplanted "the Indian plight" in the nation's headlines. Warm Springs tends to be cautious when marketing this image. It wants to look good, but not so good that fellow tribes will be jealous and fellow Oregonians will feel threatened. But it's too much to expect that the complexity and nuances of reservation life can be conveyed in a glossy annual report or in a few half-hour interviews with the media. So our view of Warm Springs and other reservations is often one-dimensional.

The preponderance of distorted popular images of American Indians, whether well-meaning or vicious, is born of such shorthand observing and reporting. Think of some those images: for the nineteenth century humanitarian, it was the helpless, downtrodden Indian children, unable to improve their lot without white charities; for the counterculture youth of the 1960s, it was the Indian as the ultimate environmentalist and tribalist; in the movies it is the gray-haired grandfather uttering monosyllabic wisdom. Such sentimental views are balanced by the typical "bordertown" prejudices: Indians as backward, belligerent, lazy, and drunk, with a "good one" being a fluke; or Indians getting fat and happy on the government "dole," sitting idly on top of a wealth of minerals, rivers, and arable land. Simplistic impressions thrive on ignorance and separation; they wither in the face of compassion and engagement.

The fifty-two portraits in this book are windows to the Warm Springs Reservation, to all reservations, and to all small communities. On an intimate, one-to-one basis, these individuals offer themselves not just as reservation Indians but as human beings with universal

concerns and pleasures. Invited to think of Indians as "people" and the reservation as a "community," readers have the opportunity to become immersed in the life of Warm Springs and to begin to look and think from the inside out.

The historical portion of this book satisfies the need for context, for an anchor to secure the faces in a particular place and time. "The Faces" introduces the people in a subjective way; "The Reservation" answers many of the inevitable questions arising from these individual encounters. As tempting as it is to think of the Warm Springs people and other reservation Indians as Americans no different from the rest, it is difficult to truly understand and empathize until we know some-thing about their history, the special terms by which they live in this country, and their cultural foundations.

Warm Springs revealed itself to me layer by layer, face by face, year by year. Sometimes it was a slow and subtle process, other times abrupt and wrenching. What was understood one day was often contradicted the next, as the people and community kept shifting in and out of focus, extending intimacies and withdrawing them, and asking to be handled delicately.

It is the same with this book. I pass along what I know about Warm Springs in the way it was delivered to me. It takes some patience. Conclusions tend to be elusive. After twelve years with Warm Springs, I still never know what face it will show me next.

THE FACES

AWAY FROM THE THRONGS of non-Indian huckleberry pickers at High Rock, Ellen and Lillie quietly harvested the purple-red fruit for the annual feast at HeHe Longhouse. Now and then the old friends exchanged a few Indian words and laughed. The Sahaptin language—soft, throaty, and sibilant—seemed suited to the windswept slopes and rolling clouds. ☐ Autumn was in the air that August day, chilling the bones and sending waves of heavy mist, but Ellen and Lillie paid no attention. Their fingers nimbly worked the dripping bushes and their legs carried them like mountain goats over the steep, rocky terrain. Never a wheeze nor a complaint issued from the sturdy old women, and never did they reward themselves with a single *wiwanu*. Tasting the berry is taboo until the feast is over and the Creator has been thanked. ☐ It could have been 1878 as well as 1978. There is a timeless quality about the traditional food gathering of the Warm Springs people. But it was the twentieth century that had brought Ellen and Lillie to the berry patch in a Dodge van instead of by horse and wagon, and had provided them with rubbers to put on over their moccasins. It was modern forest management that had squeezed out the reservation huckleberries, forcing ceremonial pickers to compete for berries on U.S. Forest Service clearcuts. Said Ellen bitterly, "One year we had to buy berries for feast. White people are making money from our Indian foods." ☐ Untying the *wapas* from her hip, Ellen packed fir boughs on the berries, laced up the basket, and hoisted it into the van. Tying on another wapas, she stooped to her work and a century slipped away again. ☐ *Postscript: In the summer of 1982, Bureau of Indian Affairs foresters launched a program to rehabilitate traditional huckleberry patches on the reservation.*

ELLEN SQUIEMPHEN

1978

H E GREW UP just like everyone else on the reservation in the days when electricity and plumbing were a luxury and all the roads were unpaved and rutted. On the ranch at Dry Hollow, his grandparents Annie and Wesley taught him to survive by raising livestock, catching fish, and picking berries. They also preached the value of education, responsibility, and commitment. There began Ken Smith's long journey to Washington, D.C., where he served four years as the Assistant Secretary of the Interior for Indian Affairs. ☐ Relaxing in his air-conditioned home on the Deschutes River, after ceremonially throwing the switch for the Tribes' new hydroelectric project, the former general manager of the Confederated Tribes reflected on his community's financial successes. "Economic development is good, but you have to be able to deal with it," said Smith, who guided the reservation's corporate interests for twelve years. "Tribal members need help and assistance to become self-sufficient, and yet, too many tribal freebies promotes dependency. We're doing the same thing the federal government did for two hundred years." He paused to think. "You know, if things got real bad around here, the only ones that would survive are the elders because they know how to provide for themselves." ☐ In the Capitol, Smith assigned himself the unpopular task of nudging tribes down the road to self-sufficiency. "To be really self-governing, tribes can't have their strings pulled by the federal government. They have to realize that it's not the government's *money* they need, but their help in strengthening the capabilities of Indian governments." When Smith began trimming the Bureau of Indian Affairs budget, merging area offices and eliminating some Indian schools, many reservation leaders felt betrayed. Warm Springs remained faithful, but the native son admits, "I think I had some of our councilmen scratching their heads a little bit when I was saying we had to rely more on the private sector for our financing." ☐ Back in Oregon, with a home in Portland as well as Warm Springs, Smith himself has joined the private sector as an economic development consultant to tribes—including his own. Having learned from Warm Springs that careful calculations and cost analyses are not the whole solution, the accountant also spends some time considering bigger questions. "As I mature," Smith says, "I ask myself, 'Where is our tribe going and where will we be in twenty or a hundred years?'" The Wasco from Dry Hollow hopes to remove some of the uncertainty from that future.

KEN SMITH

1982

FROM HER SCAFFOLD over Sherars Falls on the Deschutes River, Ellen Heath dips her net into a hole Coyote made long ago as a resting place for his ark. She knows where the spot is because her ancestors described it in petroglyphs on the river wall. ☐ Coyote's hole offers up an occasional sixty-pound salmon, while the sports fishermen downstream watch enviously. Ellen dries or cans her fish for her family, gives some away, or trades it for other necessities. "If someone comes along with a dollar and they don't have anything to trade, I'll sell it," she says, certain she's not in violation of the Tribes' subsistence fishing policy. It's the "hobo fishermen" who use her scaffold at night that are the violators, Ellen feels. "Rules after rules, they've broken every one of them. Their old people never taught them." ☐ Ellen was a child of the Columbia River, where her family had forty-nine scaffolds at Celilo Falls. Her mother had gone into business with a white man who ran a fish wheel, but their bread and butter still came from the traditional nets and traps. When Ellen wasn't attending Catholic boarding school, her old people were teaching her an ancient way of life. "I learned to dip the minute I was strong enough to hold the dip net," she said. She came to know the rhythms of the river and its inhabitants, the proper times to harvest, and the importance of approaching the river respectfully. "The river people were very cooperative. Like my mother said, 'We all got to eat, we all got to have moccasins, we all got to have beaded things.'" ☐ Greed came years later in the form of The Dalles Dam, Ellen believes. "The white man wanted brighter lights in his home and the Indians wanted money. That's the only reason the dam is there." Yet Ellen realizes that part of what keeps her alive is the wisely invested settlement the Tribes received when the fishing grounds were flooded in 1957. "Now the bonus every year is the only happiness I got. If you take away my bonus, you'll see me out there with a little cup, just beggin'." ☐ A few fish from Sherars and the Columbia, stipends for committee work, and a benevolent tribal government: Ellen's wealth is measured not in currency but in memories. ☐

Postscript: Ellen suffered a massive stroke in 1984, confining her to a wheelchair. But she is determined to fish again.

ELLEN HEATH

1982

AMOS' HEART STOPPED one November evening at a range committee meeting in the Simnasho Longhouse, in the very spot where he was later dressed in white buckskin and wrapped in Pendleton blankets. At the funeral, it was strange not to hear the soft familiar voice over the microphone, not to see the straight-backed figure in the line of drummers. As he lay there in his pine box, we all thought about his quiet simple life. ☐ A direct descendant of the treaty-signer Sim-tus-tus, Amos had been chief of the Warm Springs tribe for the last fifteen years. His passing was a state occasion, bringing the governor of Oregon and dignitaries from many Northwest tribes to Simnasho to pay their respects. ☐ I met Amos at Alice's Restaurant when I served him a bowl of cold soup, which he gently but firmly sent back. His bluish, cataract-clouded eyes and faint smile gave his face an enigmatic look. I saw him often—striding erectly into a meeting room in jeans and western shirt, standing proudly in his ceremonial buckskins and headdress at public functions, or hunched over the Tribal Council table peering with difficulty at a stack of papers. Amos seemed aloof, but not unapproachable. He would always take the time with me to explain a community feeling, a tribal tradition, or a personal opinion. When it came to getting publicity in *Spilyay Tymoo* about the National Indian Cattlemen's Association, he was uncharacteristically aggressive. ☐ He'd once been an active rancher, but had made politics a full-time occupation. As chief, he had a lifelong seat on Tribal Council, and also served on the Council's range, water, and cultural heritage committees. His involvement in regional and national Indian organizations and on the Bicentennial Commission meant a lot of traveling, but Amos managed to escape the "Holiday Inn-dian" epithet. He shunned hotel bars, was in his delegate's chair when meetings started, and returned to his reservation with copious notes and information for his Simnasho constituents and fellow councilmen. ☐ "Amos set an example for us in his work, which has to be carried out," said a younger colleague at his funeral. More than grand schemes and brilliant oratory, Amos offered this model of a dedicated statesman.

AMOS SIMTUSTUS

1979

"AH, SPILYAY WOMAN, ha, ha, ha!" would boom a voice from the driver's seat of the ancient hoodless pickup truck parked at Macy's Store. The name she had chosen for me amused her greatly, and I'd laugh along with her, secretly wondering how she navigated her truck the five miles from her home up the Tenino Valley. But then, the nearly blind and mostly deaf old woman had always been independent; as a young woman she had been the first on the reservation to wear silk stockings and to own and drive a car—so the stories go. □ I went out to Mary's place one day to photograph her as a gift for a mutual friend. It was shortly before her old cluster of houses made way for the pre-fab home her son was having built for his family. She was amused by my hour-long pursuit, and I was confounded by her spontaneous giggle every time the shutter clicked. I could only guess that she suspended her hearing problem whenever an opportunity for a laugh came up. □ I'd also heard many stories about her reign of terror as the community whiplady. Misbehaving children in the Presbyterian Church, when threatened with removal to the back pew, would settle down quickly when they saw Mary back there snapping her belt in anticipation. □ In the same church in 1979, we filed past Mary's open casket to gaze at the face that had moved us to laugh, cower, and now, mourn.

MARY HOTE

1978

F I DON'T HAVE THE FREEDOM to try new things, I get bored," says Cece. That and a desire for "financial independence" were what brought her to the law library at Lewis and Clark College. Similar urges drew her away from law school to start Whitewolf Custom Photographic Services and pursue a master's in business administration. But something more than variety and independence keep bringing her back to law. ☐ Ever since she met an Indian woman attorney at a water law conference in 1972, Cece has visualized herself practicing law in some form. "Law is the main connector between the tribes," she observed during her first year in law school. "It has made them realize how similar they are but also how different. They're all sovereigns dealing with the federal government, but federal law doesn't apply to all tribes in the same way." Cece imagined becoming a lobbyist in Washington, D.C. ☐ There was also a little ego involved, Cece admits. But most of that was satisfied during the months she clerked in the off-reservation offices of the tribal attorneys. "That job gave the people on the reservation, the group that is most important to me, the perception that I was an attorney. I've been treated by them with the respect given to a person with an advanced education." But the job also made her wonder if practicing law might, after all, be a bit boring. ☐ Fall term 1985 found Cece back at Lewis and Clark. The credentials—the degree and the "bar card"—are not as important as they were and D.C. doesn't hold the fascination it once did. Disillusioned with the kind of corporate law that is practiced at the tribal level, Cece has come to identify with "the little guy." One day a week she works as a legal aide in the Tribal Court, and she dreams about "getting the little old ladies together to incorporate their traditional values into our law and order code." Maybe Cece doesn't like to call attention to it, but there's some altruism mixed up with her keen desire for independence. Together, these impulses may be enough to place the Tribes' first law degree in Cece's hands.

CELESTE WHITEWOLF

1982

LONG BEFORE OLD LADY XNITA was immortalized with Kah-Nee-Ta Resort and Spa, Lillie Heath was a frequent visitor to the Warm Springs River and its gentle valley. She and other reservation women washed their families' clothes in the hot springs where Kah-Nee-Ta Village now stands. "It was good sitting in the water and washing," said Lillie. "Seems like when things are natural, then they fix it up and ruin them." Now the springs are the fenced-in source of hot mineral water for an Olympic-size pool and rows of tubs, designed to soothe the bodies of latterday visitors to the valley. Lillie never goes to the private bathhouse the Tribes built for their own people, even though she lives just a little way down the valley where the Warm Springs River flows into the Deschutes. ☐ The Simnasho-born woman started wintering along the Warm Springs River in 1948, helping her husband Nathan drive their cattle down when the springs at Simnasho iced up. Now Lillie lives year-round at the mouth of the river, near where she used to ford the Deschutes on her little black horse to go to the store. ☐ The neighborhood has changed, but Lillie has adapted. As one of the most-photographed women on the reservation, she has lured magazine and newspaper readers to Kah-Nee-Ta with ads that show her tending a glowing barbecue fire or hefting a Thanksgiving platter. And she shares thirty-five dollars with her friend Ellen when they're asked to butcher and barbecue salmon for Kah-Nee-Ta Lodge guests. Salmon bakes can be tests of Lillie's patience—it would be easy to lose a finger to the butcher knife while distracted by camera lenses and "funny questions, especially from those people who come from Germany and places like that." But, ever the cordial host, Lillie welcomes people to her valley, just as Xnita did generations ago.

LILLIE HEATH

1982

FOR A DOZEN YEARS, Maxine smoothly and diplomatically fielded all manner of phone calls, letters, and visitors requesting access to the highest levels of tribal management. She responded with equal care to grade school students' wide-ruled queries about life on the reservation and the more persistent questioning of the media. For untold numbers of non-Indians who reached out to the reservation, Maxine Clements *was* the Confederated Tribes. ☐ That's why it was so surprising to hear Max say, "I've always had a chip on my shoulder. It was instilled in me to distrust white people." Somewhere along the line, the executive secretary to the Tribes' general manager must have decided that the best offense was a polished telephone voice, a wealth of information, and an always-ready-to-help attitude. ☐ Max has dreamed, debated, and worked through crises with many of the reservation's leaders and their allies in the outside world. This has made her particularly sensitive to the quality of the information that gets out to the public. "We want to project an honest image, but we should also be going out and selling the Tribe to people who can benefit us." Max has grown tired of "bad press," especially over money issues. "We go along and try to provide for our people as best we can and we have a strong sense of pride in using our own money for development. But the feeling on the outside is that we're greedy." She has come to believe that local talent should be handling public relations for the Tribes. "Sometimes it really galls me to refer somebody to a P.R. office in Portland when we have people here to handle it," she said. ☐ Perhaps she took on too much of that herself. In the spring of 1985 she had a classic "burn-out" and left the pressures of the management office to put her life back together. Now Max is working on special projects for the Tribes—research and record-keeping that she never had time to do with the phones ringing all the time. She's not on the front line anymore, but that's not necessarily where the tribal image is made.

1984

When a dancer's eagle feather accidentally drops to the ground at a pow-wow, it is often Grant Waheneka who conducts the required ceremony. Placing the feather in the middle of the arena, Grant calls for a special dance to the Warriors Song. Then he asks if a fellow veteran will step to the microphone and recount a combat experience. Only then can the powwow resume. It is the perfect role for Grant. Equally comfortable in military and tribal regalia, he has served in both worlds with dignity. ☐ During his twenty-one years in the Air Force, Waheneka quickly rose to the rank of master sergeant, passing up men with more education and more engineering experience. "Since I was an Indian, I had two strikes against me. I felt I had to prove to my superiors that I could do a better job than anyone else," he said. For his last assignment, in a career that included duty as a flight engineer on a B-29 over Korea, Sergeant Waheneka was designing curriculum as part of a project that he couldn't discuss even with his wife and son. It was a training manual later used by the original seven American astronauts. ☐ In those days of invisible Indians, Grant never thought to hide his reservation origins. Wherever he went, his buckskins were ready and his ear cocked for the beat of the powwow drum. He couldn't wait to get back to his own people. "Every time I came home on leave, someone would ask me, 'When are you coming back to work for us?'" remembered Grant. ☐ Retiring from the service in 1963, he settled back into reservation life, fixing up an old house for his family and mending fences on his farm. Two years later he was elected to Tribal Council. During his six-year tenure, the Council purchased a sawmill, built a lodge and convention center at Kah-Nee-Ta, extended electricity and phones to the rural parts of the reservation, and started an education loan and grant program for the young people. In his last year, Chairman Waheneka hand-carried to Washington, D.C. a bill for the return of the disputed McQuinn Strip acreage. He was voted off Council before Congress approved the new reservation boundaries. Younger tribal voters apparently couldn't see what an "old man" who had lived off the reservation for twenty years had to offer. ☐ There is always someone seeking Grant's experience, whether it's the governor offering him a seat on a state commission, a congressman wanting help on an environmental bill, the Tribal Council needing a committeeman, or a bereaved family in Montana asking him to officiate at their giveaway. Waheneka, whose voice quavers when he speaks of such honors, always says "yes," gets into his Winnebago, and goes off to serve.

GRANT WAHENEKA

1986

I T NEVER OCCURRED to Bob Macy as a boy growing up on the reservation that he could manage the mill down the road from his father's store. Only white men held such positions in Warm Springs. But with some prodding from mentors, Bob began to see that the job could be his if he wanted it. After college, a stint in the Bureau of Indian Affairs forestry department, some time in Macy's Store, and a term on Tribal Council, Bob realized he did want it. Now he is the general manager of Warm Springs Forest Products Industries, a tribal enterprise employing more than three hundred people. □ As other Indians in tribal management have discovered, success is a mixed blessing. Some have resorted to unlisted phone numbers to ward off complaints and threats, others have sought solace in alcohol when the pressure has become too great. Bob has grown philosophical. "As a tribal member, you're more open to criticism. You're under the scrutiny of a lot of individuals with a vested interest in this plant. Hell, I'm just a kid who was down the block a few years back and there's always that standard rule: if you're not from over fifty-five miles away, you don't know anything." □ Still, Macy's arrival at the top was greeted with great expectations. "When I was appointed general manager, a Council member told me, 'Good, I'm glad to see you in that position. Now the first thing we have to do is start getting rid of the white people down there.' The pressure is on to convert the thing to all Indian employees, but it's not going to be an overnight transition." □ Because the reservation will always be his home, Bob shares the concerns of fellow tribal members, who own both the mill and the forest. "We're looking at a long-term existence here in a confined area. Right now the Tribe relies on the timber resource pretty heavily. In time it would be nice to see the Tribe reduce the mill's impact on the tribal budget. These last two years really point out how vulnerable the Tribe is to the market." □ Macy feels what may be needed is a whole change of attitude. "We have the false impression that the Tribe can take care of us and all our needs. Private enterprise should be encouraged out here. It's not necessary that the Tribe has to be in control of the operation of every enterprise. It takes away the personal incentive. □ "If we could go back twenty years and redirect our thinking, the young people could have a totally different outlook on themselves."

ROBERT MACY, SR.

1982

EVEN AS A LIFEGUARD at the Kah-Nee-Ta pool, Frank had shown signs of being a proprietor. Hulking in the mist that rises off the mineral water on winter nights or standing tall in the heat of the high desert sun, Frank felt proud to be representing the tribal resort. He was often the tourists' only link to the people of the reservation and he liked to answer their questions, correct their misconceptions. ☐ Frank and his brothers and sisters grew up with Kah-Nee-Ta in their backyard; it was a short step from Charley canyon to the resort personnel office. At thirteen, Frank signed on as a busboy, working his way up to pool manager and staring straight into a career in resort management. Then, after ten years, he quit. "Politics," he explained in a word. "Seemed like the employees were watching each other more than looking out for the guests." ☐ Out of work for two years, Frank got restless. Lifting weights wasn't enough for someone accustomed to working fourteen to sixteen hours a day. That's how Charley's Market was born. From the ground up, Frank and his brother Russell dreamed the log store and gas station into existence—a first for Simnasho and a first for a tribal member. ☐ When they went to Tribal Council with their plans, the brothers found themselves bucking a long tradition of tribal, not individual, enterprise, and a natural distrust of their youthful ambitions. But they persisted, using family acreage as collateral on a tribal loan and leaning on their instinct when experience fell short. "I didn't want to be arrogant," said Frank. "I'm still young and respectful of my elders." ☐ Over the counter at Charley's Market, Frank will still be greeting the public as he did by the pool, but instead of selling the reservation to tourists the Simnasho proprietor will be selling bread, gas, and the notion of private business to his own people.

FRANK CHARLEY

1981

SABELLE PAUSED from her rootdigging and straightened her back, gazing across Webster Flat. Perhaps she was looking for her daughter Kate, whose digging had taken her over a rise. Perhaps she was listening to the meadowlark that had earlier sung to her in Sahaptin, "You have a runny nose!" Or, perhaps she had lapsed into another reverie about her long life, recalling events that seemed to get clearer as the present faded. ☐ The sage-scented April wind penetrated her thick layers of clothing. Isabelle sighed and bent to her work again. Her sharp eyes sought the tiny green shoots of *piyaxi* and the waving stalks of *xoush*. With her iron *kapn*, the old woman pried up a clod of hard, rocky earth, revealing little tubers. Breaking the earth apart, she shook the roots free and deposited them in her bag. Immature roots she gently pressed back into the earth and told, "You keep growing now! I'll come back for you later." ☐ As she ambled across the rocky ground, stopping and leaning on her kapn now and then, Isabelle remembered riding to the fields with her mother on horseback, taking a dog along to fend off the rattlesnakes. She thought of how other women had envied her because her husband had a knack for finding good root grounds. The solitude of her digging let her mind wander over the tragedies, too—the son lost to an automobile wreck, the other daughter and rootdigging companion lost to cirrhosis. She thought sadly about more recent setbacks—the theft of her firewood by a relative, the slowness of her body. ☐ By the next rootdigging season, Isabelle had slowed even more. She'd moved in with Kate for awhile after injuring her head in a car accident, but she missed her pine thicket in Simnasho and her dog Squally, who called her "Mom," so Kate had moved her back. Rootdigging for Isabelle that year was good therapy, said Kate—a chance to feel the wind and the earth, the healthy soreness of muscles, and the fullness of many seasons of roots. ☐ *Postscript: That spring was Isabelle's last digging. In the summer, Kate held a giveaway to express her happiness that "Mom's still with us." Isabelle's memory worsened, her appetite waned, and she died two years later—the victim of Alzheimer's Disease.*

ISABELLE KEO

1981

IRENE COMES HOME from a noontime potluck, her hair cascading in careful curls and accented with a flower. She hurries into her tidy and spacious trailer, flings her purse onto an afghan-covered sofa, and heads for the sliding glass doors in the back. Kicking off her open-toed shoes, she slips into a waiting pair of rubber boots and strides across the muddy lot behind the trailer. A tribal policeman has come to check brands on the cattle she's selling. The two look over the herd and converse at the pasture gate. She's all business, even when she's tossing her long hair, wrinkling her nose, and giving in to her high-pitched giggle. ☐ "A lot of women give me a bad time about my farming," says Irene when she's back inside and settled into a chair. "But that's because their husbands tease them. 'Look at Irene out there helping Jack,' they say. But then, lots of other women help their husbands, too. And some women even farm by themselves." ☐ It's certainly no sacrifice for Irene. "I enjoy it," she says. "It's different, instead of just staying in the house and taking care of it. It's dirty work, but then I grew up in potato fields and berry patches. Once in a while I rode on my dad's hay wagon and tromped the hay down." Now, Irene is in charge of mowing and raking her eighty-five acres of feed grain, a job made even more enjoyable when the old tractor was replaced by an air-conditioned, stereo-equipped cab. ☐ When Irene married Jack, a Midwesterner, they sold most of Irene's cattle and operated the Mobil station in Warm Springs for a time. Then Jack bought a logging truck, eventually becoming truck shop supervisor at the mill, while Irene became a popular waitress and bartender. "I'm done with that phase of my life," she says firmly. "I'm into farming now." Fifteen years ago they started building up their herd again, and now Jack and Irene are "just beginning to show a little profit." ☐ Living the life of the independent farmer, Irene didn't have much to do with tribal affairs until she was appointed to the Council's recreation and education committees a few years ago. "Before the committees, I didn't even know anything about the treaty. I just lived day to day and didn't think about politics. Now I'm kind of excited about the things that will happen in the future of this reservation." ☐ Friends tried to talk Irene into running for Tribal Council in 1983, but she declined. "If I get involved, I want to be really involved. But when the farm work's gotta be done, it's gotta be done!" And for someone who thinks that "just going out to check the cattle is fun," the fields would always be beckoning.

IRENE TOWE

1981

JACOB FRANK SITS on the corral post and looks over the herd of wild horses rounded up the day before. "That guy got out last night? Too wild, I guess . . . Leggy little sorrel, init? . . . Hey, there's Smoke Signals—only buckin' horse left on this end of the reservation. Yeah, he's a cute one—kind of a Romeo." ☐ The North End's hundreds of wild horses are individuals to Jacob, recognizable from season to season by their temperaments as well as their markings. Horses are his business. He is a livestock owner, a Council-appointed horse ride boss, and an aide for the Oregon State University extension service. He rides them, rounds them up, brands them, tests their blood, breaks them, sells them, or sits quietly and observes them. Horses are his passion, too, a symbol of what has been good in his life. "You watch the horses running free and it relaxes you," he says. "They're a beautiful sight—free as the breeze." ☐ It pleases Jacob that his son Yahtin has taken up training and riding racehorses. "They're teaching each other to be aggressive, competitive, and responsible. These things you have to learn in order to live within life itself. A lot of Indians back away from this." ☐ Jacob knows because he spent the first half of his own life "backing away." He left home at age twelve, weary of life in Simnasho where he shared two rooms with seven people and suffered the label "hillbilly" at boarding school. Away from home, he fell into drinking and fighting, a life-style that climaxed when he "worked over" a cop and wound up at McNeil Island federal penitentiary in Washington. ☐ "Booze will make you hurt the things you like in life," says a wiser Jacob, who admits sadly that alcohol had even led him to abuse the animals he loved. "When I reached twenty-five years old, all that wild hair was gone. Then I thought, 'I think that's about enough for one man.'" A Presidential Pardon helped him get on track. Then in 1977, he was elected to Tribal Council. "I saw it as being accepted back by my people," he says. ☐ For reservation boys who show signs of becoming "another Jacob Frank all over again," the horseman offers this prescription: "If you're wanting a lot of excitement, getting too high and mighty, go ride that colt." Through his drumming group and his summer work crews, Jacob has tried to pass on to a few boys some of the grace and confidence he has learned during a life astride the horse.

JACOB FRANK, SR.

1982

WHEN THE MUSIC IS ON, the memories are vivid. Frankie Laine on KRCO, the Saturday night dances in the dorms at the boarding school, the jitterbug contests that he won regularly. ☐ Then it all gets fuzzy. The "lost years" he calls them. At first the "boozing" was fun—the twenty-first birthday party, the youthful camaraderie. Twenty years later Peter woke up and realized his life was a bad joke. He owned nothing: "All the money I spent on booze, I coulda had a mansion, with Cadillacs." He couldn't hold a job: "Who the hell wanted to work? I got per capita." He had no family: "I'd call my mother and sister and they'd give me heck. I stopped calling." The parks near Burnside Street in Portland were his home: "You're not gonna spend your last few dollars on a room when you gotta have that drink first thing in the morning." Even the music had changed. No one was jitterbugging anymore. ☐ He tried to turn it around at Eastern Oregon State Hospital in 1972. "But I wasn't getting the help I really needed. They were just putting me in these places to get me off the streets." At the Tribes' Recovery House, where a bed was always ready for him, Peter had the most success. He was even house manager for a time in 1980. ☐ As he watched the ball drop at Times Square on the eve of 1982, Peter resolved not to have a drink during the coming year. "I'm not going to brag around about being sober," he said a couple of months into the year, "but I'll tell you, I can get mad now without having to get drunk." While he is taking life "one day at a time"—the Alcoholics Anonymous way—Peter is thinking about his future. He still wants to be the baker he'd trained to be while at Chemawa Indian school. He dreams of one day directing the Tribes' alcohol program. And as soon as he gets out of the Recovery House, he wants to hold a jitterbug contest, for old times' sake. ☐ *Postscript: The last time I saw Peter, he was worried; his speech was slurred even when he was sober. Then in early 1987, I saw a funeral notice on the door of Macy's Store. Peter's music had stopped.*

PETER REED

1982

WOVEN INTO VIOLA'S WILLOW BASKETS are the quiet of Seekseequa canyon and her memories of livelier days on the "south end" of the reservation. As she strips the willows she gathered in a meadow along Seekseequa Creek, Viola remembers a community full of basketmakers, Paiutes most of them. On Sundays they faithfully attended the Seekseequa Church, now weathered and idle; as soon as the visiting pastor was out of sight, they would pull out their stick game sets for a long afternoon of gambling. Then the fire of 1938 and a changing economy left the canyon quiet and the willows untouched for many years. ☐ As a Wasco child growing up in another reservation valley, Viola had watched her grandmother work baskets. But it wasn't until she married Nick and moved to their new home at Seekseequa that she learned to strip and weave the tricky willow. One teacher, a Paiute woman from Nevada, was rewarded with many gifts for her efforts. Still, it took a while to master the techniques. When Viola's brother Felix examined her first basket, he remarked with a glint in his eye that it sure looked like the work of an old blind basketmaker who used to live at Seekseequa. ☐ Now Viola has a lot of orders to fill. She knows the good willows from the "funny" ones and the right time to gather them. She once broke a tooth off her denture while stripping willow branch, and her wrist often stiffens from arthritis. The work is slow, especially when a visitor comes to listen to her soft reminiscing. ☐ *Postscript: Nick, who had become the Paiute chief in 1975, died in 1985. That winter Viola put aside her baskets to make quilts and tule mats for the memorial giveaway. She knew the willows would be there when she was ready for them.*

VIOLA KALAMA

1981

T<small>HIS WAS HER FIRST GIVEAWAY</small> and she was trying to do it right. After so many deaths in her family, Alice felt compelled to deal with these two—her eldest children—as traditionally as possible. Here she was at the Pi-Ume-Sha powwow, months after Joyce had died of cancer and Fabian had followed in a car wreck, memorializing them in public with a salmon dinner and a giveaway. ☐ She felt the eyes of the community upon her: modern Alice Florendo, rarely seen in a wingdress but often seen in the company of white friends. It didn't help to explain that she grew up with her Wasco grandmother, a traditional healer, and that many of the old ways were bubbling up into her consciousness now that she was a great-grandmother herself. She sought counsel from longhouse people for some of the details of her memorial. Then she nervously awaited the criticism that didn't come. ☐ "Alice is in the process of becoming an elder," an off-reservation friend of hers said quite simply. She qualifies for the Tribes' senior citizen benefits, that's true. Her high blood pressure and swarms of small strokes tell her she's not young anymore. Marrying as a teenager and losing two husbands and three children has made her feel old at times. But being an elder is something else altogether. There are certain expectations. An elder in Warm Springs is looked to as a mirror on the past, an archive of cultural and historical information, a model of morality, a source of wisdom. It is no wonder Alice feels some pressure to gather up the teachings of her own elders, to reconcile her white and Indian impulses, to speak Wasco more fluently, to tell the Coyote stories she learned from her grandmother. ☐ And she sews, putting away shawls, wingdresses, and ribbon shirts for those occasions when her relatives need an elder to lean on. ☐ *Postscript: Alice had a massive stroke in April 1986 and had to put her sewing aside. During her slow recovery, she's had to learn how to lean on her family.*

ALICE FLORENDO

1983

FOR YEARS, MAGGIE WAVED my camera away, saying, "No pictures!" But she didn't see me while she was absorbed in a game of *jejewai* during the Pi-Ume-Sha powwow and I knew I could finally record her striking Paiute face. As I had suspected, her reasons for avoiding cameras were not traditional or spiritual. Later when she looked at the picture, she laughed, shook her head and said, "I look so ugly! All wrinkled!" ☐ The ninety-four-year-old woman stubbornly resists old age and ignores relatives' suggestions that she quit traveling to stick game tournaments to gamble. "You want me to stay home," she tells them "you put a dollar in my hand." Maggie supplements her tribal pension and social security checks with her winnings, while the fun she has gambling probably adds years to her life. "You feel good when you go to a different place," she said, "instead of like a prisoner." ☐ It's hard for her to sit idle with an arthritic knee after a life of physical work. Before she was married, Maggie cooked at the rooming house for government employees and cleaned up after the boys at the boarding school dormitory. Sometimes her parents hitched a team to a wagon, ferried across the Deschutes River, and delivered Maggie to homes in Prineville and Willowdale where she kept house for non-Indian families. ☐ When she married Sam Wewa, Maggie tried her hand at wheat and potato farming on the South End. She remembers walking behind a horse-drawn plow and hauling and shocking hay before the sun got too hot. Trips into Warm Springs to get groceries were made on horseback or by hack. It was a day-long ride on rutted roads that meant camping out at a relative's place and starting back in the morning. ☐ Now Maggie is too old even to gather her own Indian foods. "I'm a retired rootdigger," she said resignedly. She has to buy her roots and berries now. Gambling gives her some of the cash to do it.

MAGGIE WEWA

1981

I F A FINANCIAL CRISIS COMES UP in the Switzler family—there's no cash for groceries or one of the kids sends for money to get home from somewhere—Maxine packs up a few pieces of beadwork and takes them to Kah-Nee-Ta or the tribal gift shop. She knows that if they're buying at all, they'll buy her work. ☐ Maxine's famous beadwork comes out of a chaotic corner of her linoleum-floored living room, a squirrel's nest of strung beads, loose beads, thread, bits of flannel and buckskin, scraps of paper bearing design sketches, and a telephone. Using primarily "cut beads"—tiny faceted beads made only in Czechoslovakia—she meticulously crafts buckles, watchbands, medallions, moccasins, horse trappings, and even occasional letter openers or salt and pepper shakers. Her work is tight, even, bright, and pretty. People want more of it than she can supply. ☐ "I do it because it's a pleasure," said Maxine. "I know Delton could provide for me." Her husband, a cattle rancher, initially felt threatened by her income but now he helps out on some of the simpler pieces. Sometimes the two will take her earnings from her jewelry box and head south for a lark in Reno, doing some trading along the way (or some selling on the way back if their luck wasn't too good). ☐ Maxine has resisted the urge to get overly businesslike in her beadworking. "I don't want to be commercialized, making a whole bunch of one pattern. To me each rose or eagle is a challenge to see how real I can make it look. Each one is different." There are compromises, of course. "It's hard to make the eagle feather designs look different, but those silly feathers is what's moving out!" She'll also do Mickey Mouse if she has to, but she does draw the line firmly on two requests: marijuana paraphernalia and pictures of nude women. "I told one person, 'No way! I'll make you a man, in 3-D even, but I won't make a nudie lady!'" ☐ Maxine always wonders where her beadwork ends up, but sometimes she knows all too well. When someone asked her to make a belt buckle to be presented to then-Secretary of the Interior James Watt, she thought to herself, "Oh, too bad, my beadwork will be full of tomatoes!"

1983

A T THE TIME we became acquainted, Susana was "working in a fervor," painting eight to fifteen hours a day, her unruly hair stranger to a comb, something driving her on. "I didn't want to be an artist," she said during a brief lull. "I didn't want the power, I didn't want to suffer. Why me?" ☐ She felt she had been "born as an artist" only in the last year. Finally free of the need to carry on where her artist brother Carlos had left off when he died at twenty-one, Susana now had her own vision. "Messengers from the natural world—the wind, the water, owls, coyotes" were clamoring inside her head, along with voices of the reservation's unhappy young people. All were directing her to fill canvas after canvas, to make that "connection with the universe" that would help show her the way . . . to what? "To becoming a full human being," she said simply. In the meantime, Susana knew this vision was enough to brand her as "eccentric," if not downright "radical." ☐ Susana had come back to the reservation in search of something she had lost. "Being poor was a good place to begin," she said of a childhood spent in migrant labor camps. But then, amidst the "power and money" of the San Francisco art world, Susana felt "divorced and lost from the land. Where was the art? It was back home." She became a fisherwoman at *Tlxni* (Sherar's Falls on the Deschutes River), where her family had a traditional site. Disheartening as it was to find that she couldn't make a living from fishing, there were other lessons to be learned on the scaffolds over the rushing water. "Now when I fish," Susana said, "it's to maintain our fishing grounds. And it's a pilgrimage, to offer myself to my ancestors." ☐ Her life thus far had been a "personal pilgrimage," an effort she now understood to be a balancing of the spiritual and the intellectual, the feminine and the masculine. "I have to experience both sides to reach some conclusion in my art," she said, paraphrasing something she'd read from Virginia Woolf. "I grew up streetwise in an era of dissidence," she added. "It was a male-dominated world that tended to stymie human potential. I wasn't allowed to express my feelings. Now I see that women are more in touch with their own individuality, with the Creator. My work reflects what women have taught me about nurturing and healing." ☐ So she worked feverishly, alone in her little house at Wolf Point, reaching out silently to her people and beyond. "I want to be part of a new world that's coming," she said, "a world where our people, like artists, can see through the hearts and minds of women and children and find true peace."

SUSANA SANTOS

1986

THE EMBATTLED SPACECRAFT rotates, thrusts, and fires, dodging and blasting asteroids that hurtle through video outer space. Buckwheat's fingers flutter like moths on the control buttons and his jaw drops in utter concentration. "I don't like this machine," he scowls. "The firing mechanism is screwed up." But still he amasses thousands of points and his codified name "BUK" stands unchallenged next to the 100,000-plus score at the top of the asteroids register. □ Buck knows he's the best—in a town where being the best can be a liability. The first Burger Inn asteroids tournament never got off the ground because as soon as Buckwheat signed up, all the other players erased their names and asked for their money back. Buck just shrugs. "They all think my scores are pretty awesome." It's un-Warm Springs to seek too much glory, so Buckwheat acknowledges his skill by giving due credit to nature: "I don't really have to work at it. I'm just naturally good." The champ wasn't always good. He figures he spent about ten dollars learning the game. Now he can play all day on one quarter. "I could go for the world record (seventy-eight hours) if I had a sponsor." □ Back on Earth, Buck has a few personal asteroids to battle. He's been trying to get his "good hand and eye coordination" back onto the varsity basketball court. "Two too many Fs" sidelined him, so he found some different friends, enrolled himself in the alternative education program at Warm Springs, and hopes to be back on the team for his senior year. Nothing an "awesome" asteroids player can't handle. □ *Postscript: Four years later, James was a towering young man with a GED, a sports car, and a closet full of silk trophy jackets won at Indian basketball tournaments. "They don't call me Sir Jamalot for nothing!" he told me one day as he was dunking basketballs to the sound of Mozart.*

JAMES "BUCKWHEAT" SCOTT

1982

FELIX WAS DOZING in his armchair when I knocked on the screen door. He stirred, took a swing at the circling flies, and walked stiffly across the living room to let me in. All I wanted was to ask directions to a neighbor's house, but he apparently meant to have me visit. ☐ His friends had taken off for Portland and left him behind, he said. He couldn't go anywhere because he'd snapped his key off in the ignition of his station wagon. He was thirsty in the one hundred degree weather and would soon be hungry. I had visited Felix several times before, looking for information about Indian medicine, hide tanning, and eel preparation. This time I gladly went after the ground beef, eggs, milk, KoolAid, and soda pop that he said would get him through the next couple of days. ☐ When I returned, Felix said, "You'll stay and have some pop." I stayed. We looked at the pictures on his piano and he told me about the days when he played bass fiddle with a Warm Springs dance band. I asked if he still played the piano. In answer, he pushed aside the clutter, uncovered the keyboard, and gave his all to "My Wild Irish Rose." ☐ The impromptu afternoon concert over, I was about to leave when he asked, "Do you have a typewriter?" I said I did. "Well, in case you forget to take it with you, you can keep this one in the car and you'll never be without one." He pointed to an old portable. "As long as you're working here and writing about us, you can use it. And take the box of paper there in the closet." I reached for a few sheets. "No, the whole box!" he insisted. ☐ I wanted to give him something in return—a cure for his diabetes, a fresh start on a liver, or a good pair of ears. Maybe it would just be another visit on a hot afternoon. ☐ *Postscript: Felix was found dead in his house one day in the spring of 1984, before I could return his typewriter.*

1981

EVA HAD BEEN SAVED a couple of months earlier. At the camp meeting, she testified to her brothers and sisters in her husky voice: ☐ "Praise the Lord! I want to tell you folks a story. It may not mean much to you, but I've been havin' this dental work done. The dentist did a root canal on my face, and it got infected and swollen. My lip was hangin' out like it was busted. One night, I made a fire in the stove and I was lyin' there with my old man, smokin' joint after joint to kill the pain, but I couldn't get stoned! I started sayin' a prayer of death—'God, if this is the time for you to take me then let it be. I'm a miserable woman!' Then I heard a voice callin' me and it was my friend Rose, come to take me to a doctor. That doctor stuck a long needle in my mouth and drained out all kinds of pus and blood. He said it was only an inch from my brain and I might have died that night! It was a miracle! God had spared me again—the first time was when I tried to kill myself. I guess he wanted to give me the message. Praise the Lord! I haven't had any weed or booze since then. I've been gettin' rid of the hate in me and bustin' down walls between me and my enemies. I plan to marry my old man and maybe God will help me get my daughter back. And some day I want to teach little children about Jesus." ☐ When the guitars and the preaching and the praying had electrified the atmosphere in the church, Eva shed tears—"showers of gems for Christ," as she called them later. "This is the first real thing I've ever felt real about. I'm not quittin' now!"

1981

A STOLEN NAP DURING A LULL in a longhouse funeral is all Prunie can count on when the community needs her. ☐ At the Agency Longhouse, Prunie is the leading elder of the Washat religion—bell-ringer, "Indian undertaker," teacher of tradition, and comforter. Across town in the community counseling center, she is a "traditional cultural specialist/ombudsman," performing some of the same functions for a salary. This monetary adaptation to modern times is challenged regularly at general council meetings; the existence of the job is an unwelcome reminder to some that the traditional methods for passing along the culture are eroding. ☐ "The elders are harder to approach now," says Prunie. "Many young people want to hang onto the culture, but they don't know what it is—it's just a word." Prunie provides a link between the old and the young, the Indian and the white. She is called on to explain the forgotten spiritual bases for the rituals surrounding birth, death, marriage, and the use of traditional foods and medicines. She schools non-Indian health professionals in cultural matters, encourages the use of Indian curing methods, and helps traditionals feel more comfortable with modern doctors. It was Prunie's happy discovery while studying for her associate's degree in mental health that much of what she was learning about the "white ways" had parallels in the Indian medicine she had grown up with. "Indian doctors can soothe just like drugs," she says. ☐ Prunie derives peace and strength from this bridge between the cultures. But the woman who ministers in a jogging suit and knit cap as often as a wingdress is also a source of controversy. When she modifies a longhouse ritual or videotapes a sacred ceremony, she treads on new, uncertain ground. ☐ Her position in the community—partly chosen and partly inherited (with some reluctance) from her parents—at once surrounds her with people and isolates her. Who was there to prop her up when she had to ritually dress her own son's body? She is sustained by a deep respect for her own traditional upbringing and her belief that in the old ways lie the cures for a troubled reservation.

PROSANNA "PRUNIE" WILLIAMS

1981

MATILDA RINGS THE BELL at the Simnasho Longhouse under the stern gaze of her father, the late Warm Springs Chief Frank Queahpama, whose oil portrait hangs above the tule mats. As the matriarch of Simnasho, Matilda commands respect with her own forbidding countenance, which occasionally cracks into a sparkling smile and shaking laugh. ☐ Growing up in Simnasho was simple for Chief Queahpama's daughters until it was time to go to boarding school at the Agency. There, Matilda was taunted and drawn into fights by the more modern Wasco girls, and she soon got sick and began coughing up blood. Returning to the security of her rural home, she put her books aside and learned the ways of the Simnasho chief while cooking for meetings held at her father's place. To this day, she retains a distrust of the Agency people, who came to the reservation a couple of years later than her own Tygh Valley people but learned the white man's ways faster. ☐ When her husband Louis died in 1972, Matilda reluctantly took over as bell-ringer at the longhouse. "I thought we'd have Washat only at funerals. Then a young man asked me to teach him how to drum and worship. I just cried." Matilda had grown up in the Washat tradition, learning songs that were given by God to her ancestors, and stories that told of the creation and the coming of the longhouse religion to her people. Her grandfather had been a martyred Washat leader—abducted from his tule longhouse near Kah-Nee-Ta by Catholic and Presbyterian Indians and dragged behind a horse, his flesh torn "just like Jesus." Matilda would carry on what he had died for. ☐ It is the gentleness of her family's religion that has kept Matilda faithful and active, even though Washat lacks the "power" of other reservation sects. Her husband's dabbling in the Feather religion had frightened her and she felt her own participation in Shaker services had been unwelcome. "They said I wasn't good enough to be a Shaker because I believed in Longhouse, too." ☐ There is also discord within the Washat world from time to time. Matilda and her sisters firmly promote traditions as they learned them, while another trio of sisters at the Agency have their own interpretations. A sadness can be seen in Matilda's face when there aren't enough drummers for a service. But she rings the bell anyway for the people who want to listen. ☐ *Postscript: Matilda said happily in 1984, "We're growing up now. We have seven drummers every week!" In 1985, the Tribes built a new Simnasho Longhouse, tripling the size of the original one.*

MATILDA MITCHELL

1982

INSIDE THE SMALL HOUSE at Dry Creek the energy builds, spilling out into the cool night air. Carved sticks pound the floor, voices rise with every verse sung, a woman spins in ecstasy. At the heart of the gathering, fluttering a healing eagle feather, is a small, delicate man with gray braids and a Hawaiian shirt. ☐ "I receive a gift from the Lord to help the people," explains Andrew David. "The light hits me. You can feel the whole house, it will hit the whole house, the light, just like shocks. That's when everybody makes up their mind in full faith." ☐ The light hit his great-grandfather in the last century, speaking to him and giving him the drums, feathers, and songs of a new religion. In 1919, Andrew went the way of "Nashat Ticham" and embraced the Feather religion "to keep myself in health, to forget all my sorrow feelings that I had when my father died." He has carried it on humbly ever since, almost shy about the spiritual power that has grown within him. ☐ "You know, I'm just ordinary now," he says one day. "When I stand up to help a person, when I ask the Lord—my body will feel different then. But I never brag about this religious. No-o, I'm just like way behind everybody all the time. But when my turn comes to do something, well that's the time I have to pray pretty hard for myself, then help the sick ones, bad-feelings people." ☐ When he needs help himself, he goes to others with power, like the Filipino faith healers who visited Warm Springs one summer. As Andrew's daughter Arlene told it, when they worked on the old man, angels stood protectively around him, seagulls swooped out of his body, and the healers spontaneously sang an Indian song they'd never heard before. ☐ To the growing number of people who come to his home for feasts, for worship, for healings, he insists, "You have to step in and give yourselves up so you can keep on carrying it on when I'm gone. If you don't, well it will just be too bad for all you people. You wouldn't know what to do, which way to turn. You might only believe in Devil then. You know what's happening nowadays with dopes and alcohol, that's the way you'll be." ☐ There is much to teach, so Andrew hangs onto his increasingly frail life. "It's a wonderful thing, this Feather religion," he says, still in awe of the gift he was given. ☐ *Postscript: Andrew died in Arlene's arms in August of 1986. So deep was the "lake of tears" in their house, that Arlene was unsure when services would begin again.*

ANDREW DAVID

1979

THE CANDLES AND CROSSES of the Indian Shaker church were at the center of Clarence McKinley's life, from the time he "received the Holy Ghost" in 1949 until he died thirty-five years later as state elder of the Warm Springs Shaker Church. But it was more than the healing flames, more than the hypnotic songs and bell-ringing in the white-walled church that inspired Clarence. It was the open-ended Shaker creed that gave him room to explore, to satisfy his spiritual and intellectual curiosity. ☐ "Christianity and Indian traditions say the same things and the Shaker church brings them together," said the man who sometimes received his knowledge directly from God. "The Bible was all right in the beginning, but then they began to emphasize the Ten Commandments and a lot of our people couldn't follow them. The Bible was being used to convict, not convert." The Shaker church supplied Clarence with a code of moral conduct—including abstention from drinking, smoking, gambling—but not with the right to judge others. "I can tell you how to live, but that's from me. It might not work for you." ☐ Yet people were continually dropping by Clarence's house for advice. "When he received visitors," said his son-in-law Johnny Howtopat, a fellow Shaker, "he always turned off the TV, even if his wife was watching her favorite program, and gave them his fullest attention. Through his speaking, it kind of released people from what was bothering them. It was like the Word of the Lord was going through him to the people. Of course, he wasn't without his faults. He backslid once or twice." But as Clarence himself said, "Trying to be perfect is a sin, too." ☐ A welder and timber faller by trade, and a hook-and-line fisherman by avocation, the tall, strapping man with the white crew cut attracted both white and Indian people to him. "He never taught us colors," said his daughter, Iva Pennington. "People were all the same to him." This was clear when the Shaker elder was looking for money to build a new church in the 1950s; his biggest contributors were non-Indian logging and construction companies. Suspicious of technology ("God intended something very different for us than science and modern ways"), Clarence thought it should be tempered by the traditional notions of cooperation and community. According to Iva, "His biggest dream was for the Tribes to have a vocational training center to teach children to use their hands and their heads." ☐ In Clarence, the sacred and the secular resided comfortably. "The Shaker religion has made me really understand what life is and how everything fits."

1982

HIS NAME would occasionally appear cruelly on a bathroom wall, linked with a schoolgirl's name. ☐ Then, amid raised eyebrows, Norval married a girl thirty years his junior, also described by the community as "a little slow." It was her idea to get married, said Norval, but soon Terri was gone more than home and Norval was nursing his pride by saying, "There were other women I could have had." ☐ Norval worked as a janitor until diabetes claimed his eyesight. "They led me around like a dog or a cat," said Norval, remembering the indignity of having two helpers. He lost one eye during surgery and the other shows him a blurry world. He doesn't know if he'll be able to work again. ☐ Norval feels best when he's war dancing at powwows or playing electric guitar at the Full Gospel Church. At his senior citizens duplex, which he's entitled to because of his disability, he feels a little lonely. Terri is saying she wants to marry someone else and he doesn't get many visitors. It's a long time between powwows and tent meetings.

NORVAL TUFTI

1981

AHEYA, AHEYA! Everybody get out there and show your stuff! *Everybody* dance! This is the intertribal. Get out and warm up! You make us proud . . . Tuch! Where are you, Tuch? There you are, you son of a gun, coming out from behind that bush with juniper berries all over your knees, Tuch . . . ! ☐ "Powwow time! Pi-Ume-Sha means a gathering of Indians for a good time, to carry on traditions and fellowship. Take it away, Widespot Singers! Wilfred got thirsty and went on a run, init? Take it away, Pine Grove Juniors! Hey, Spilyay photographer, here I am. You got a picture worth a fortune here . . . ☐ "Ten minutes till the Grand Entry. O.K., line up down here, single file, Injun style. Would everyone rise, please, to pay tribute to the flags. This is an Indian powwow so we use the Indian flag, the staff of many feathers, to lead the grand entry, but we must also pay respect to the flag our veterans fought under. I once heard an old man say the blue represents the blue of the sky and the stars was put there by the Creator; the white means holy, speaking the truth, peacefulness just like the white clouds or the snow which brings moisture to all living things; the red could represent the American Indian, but to the veteran it means the blood of a brother. Let's all bow our heads and pray in our own way . . . ☐ "Last call, fancy dancers twelve and under. O.K. judges, get out there. You young bucks, this is your contest. Check your dingalings, I mean your bells. I remember when Rudy and I used to jump higher than that. Now I got my weight out in front and I have to stop two-and-a-half beats before the drum stops so all of *me* is stopped . . . ☐ "At this time we'll have a blanket dance—the Indian way of passing the hat. If you have some loose change or a hundred dollar bill, we'd appreciate the donation. It costs a hell of a lot to put on a show like this . . . ☐ "Remember a few years ago there was a big party at Little Big Horn? What was that guy's name? Goldilocks? Well, let's have a honky dance in his honor—a little half-time entertainment. Don't be bashful, now, it's just for fun. War dancing isn't as easy as it looks, is it? O-o-oh, look at that one getting hot. Ugh, me Tarzan, you Jane! . . . ☐ "Rations are at eight in the morning. You men, be sure to kick your women out of your tepees and get 'em to make you some breakfast . . . ☐ "What are you waiting for, drummers? I'm just B.S.-ing here. Take it away! We got all night to go!"

NATHAN "EIGHTBALL" JIM

1978

SINGING IN THE CHOIR or playing basketball at her school in Madras, Masami reveals nothing of her life around the powwow arena. Even the friends she dances with can only guess what it feels like to be a champion. ☐ Masami was four when she first stepped out onto the Pi-Ume-Sha grounds in Warm Springs and kept perfect time to the circle dance song. It was not enough to be naturally graceful and light on her feet; Masami used her head, too. She was the first in her Wasco-Warm Springs-Japanese family to dance competitively and she had much to learn. Drummers grew accustomed to a tiny figure hovering near them, dancing in place while she absorbed subtleties in their songs and singing styles. She practiced endlessly, even down the aisles of the supermarket. ☐ When the prize money started coming in, her mom called her "champ." Tootsie sewed beautiful beaded outfits for her, using the eagle feather motif for strength, and mirrors to show onlookers what they were feeling. Sometimes the mirrors reflected the jealousy of other dancers, so Masami began staying out of some contests. Then she stopped winning at home powwows altogether and had to travel great distances to gain recognition. ☐ Among the Plains people, Masami found inspiration and stature. Medicine men wanted to be near her, drums adopted her, and one older couple took her as their granddaughter. From these people, she learned to burn sweet grass and rub the smoke into her moccasins before dancing, and to wear a medicine bag on her hip while she danced, nibbling on the herbs when she felt nervous. ☐ At home, she keeps these things to herself, even while she learns her own tribal traditions. Her relatives wonder if she is a royal ancestor come back to live with them. But most people only see in Masami a pretty girl quietly growing into a woman, a powwow champion who still loves to dance.

MASAMI DANZUKA

1978

SONNY LEARNED TO FIGHT on the asphalt playground of Warm Springs Elementary, a coming-of-age ritual among reservation kids. But he learned *when* to fight when he joined the Warm Springs Boxing Club. "I don't want bullies," says Sonny's coach, Gerald Smith. "I tell them if they've got something to prove, to get in the ring and win the national championship." ☐ Sonny has won a few titles around the Northwest, but Gerald thinks he could be national material. "It all depends on self-discipline," a trait the coach sees in short supply among the Warm Springs youth. "It's sad to see the lack of discipline and dedication, and to see natural talents wasted," says the ex-boxer. ☐ There was a time when Sonny worked out two hours a day and it paid off, both in points and in the boy's self-confidence. Early on, Sonny found a focus for his developing skills—an up-and-coming Eugene, Oregon boxer in the same weight class. "Sonny got beat every time," says Gerald, "but he hung in there. Eventually Sonny rocked him a couple of times." Sonny remembers their best bout. "We were hitting each other pretty good, getting stunned pretty good, and we'd step back and try to get out of the daze we were in and try it again. We went three rounds." The Eugene boy has since gone on to the National Junior Olympics, but Sonny is still deciding whether to stay in the ring. ☐ This fall and winter, the eighth grader has played football and wrestled with the school teams. "That's a priority," says Gerald of his boxers. "I want them to have the experience of team sports. They can always come back to the club later." ☐ So far, Sonny has kept coming back. "Boxing feels like it comes naturally to me," he says. His coach agrees. "He was born with it. He'll throw punches you've never taught him." Sonny knows it would take some work, but at fourteen he dreams of one day going professional. "I'd like to go to New England and talk to "Marvelous Marvin" Hagler—to find out how hard he trains," says the aspiring boxer. He thinks he already knows the answer. Seven years with the Warm Springs Boxing Club have shown Sonny that the passion of the playground is scant preparation for the discipline of the ring.

SONNY JACKSON

1986

LOYD SMITH SITS very quietly at the school board meetings, his silence sometimes disconcerting to his fellow board members, all of whom are white. During almost twenty years of representing Warm Springs in the Jefferson County 509-J School District, Lloyd has had a message for Madras residents: that Indian parents *do* care. They care that their children too often leave Warm Springs Elementary below the norm in language skills; that racial stereotyping on both sides makes the arrival of Indian students at Madras Junior High a tense experience; that Indian students are dropping out of high school at a much higher rate than their non-Indian counterparts. ☐ On home turf, Lloyd has another message for Indian parents. Times have changed, he tells them. The Warm Springs community can no longer depend on the whipman to keep order or on the elders to teach survival skills to the children. Parents must now be responsible for seeing that their children learn how to survive in the modern world. But the time when boarding schools and federal policy tried to "create Indians in the image of the white man" is also over. Indians now have the opportunity to influence curriculum, to ask that teachers respect students' cultural differences, and to put tribal support behind agreed-upon educational goals. "If parents understand how Indian culture conflicts with the dominant culture and also how they can blend, then they will understand how to proceed," says Lloyd. ☐ "The two communities have to meet halfway. Throwing rocks back and forth across the river doesn't work."

1981

"I N PUBLIC I TURN INTO QUEEN TRUDEE and leave the old Trudee in the car. There's a certain image that's expected. You can't be popping your gum during the Lord's Prayer." ☐ Trudee's grace is natural, but with a dozen titles to her name she's got her public image down to a science. "I did this to see if I could, now I wish I could stop. After Miss Warm Springs I decided it was all over. Then the old fire started burning again." Trudee went on to become the first runner-up to both Miss Indian North America and Miss National Congress of American Indians, taking the Miss Indian Northwest title for herself. The demands of royalty in Indian Country are great and Trudee's fire is cooling again as she refocuses on college and career. But she'll never be the same person again, and doesn't want to be. ☐ "I got out of my shyness," says Trudee. "I learned to speak and present myself better and to go for it." She had good models—her father, Rudy, is an outgoing, articulate tribal leader, her mother, Anna, a former beauty pageant winner. Trudee did get sidetracked for awhile. "When I was a freshman I got in the wrong peer group. I was naive then and what they said, I always did. It resulted in me finally getting kicked out of school. I was a little hood! My parents really watched me that year and made me go everywhere they went—to Sunday services at the longhouse, to powwows. That's how I met Jacob (her boyfriend, and later her husband). Then I found out there was more to life than going out and getting high." ☐ Many of her contemporaries haven't discovered that yet. They opt for fast cars and alcohol to bolster their poor self-images, says Trudee. "They're trying to be something, trying to be proud, trying to prove something. They don't think of themselves as able to do things. Not enough people give them support. It's kind of like a cage they can't get out of: the door's there but there's a jungle outside." ☐ Out in the jungle, Trudee sometimes feels alone. "Your own people are the hardest to please," she observes. Accustomed to being called down for her successes, she insists, "I don't let no one make me feel inferior."

TRUDEE CLEMENTS

1981

IT'S JUST A HAND-ROLLED CIGARETTE," Packy tells friends when they see this photograph tacked on the living room wall of his townhouse apartment. In any case, it wasn't lighted—not during the half-hour I spent visiting with trusties at the tribal jail. Packy was nineteen at the time, doing thirty days for parole violation. It was a stage in his life when he was so busy having a good time that he didn't know it was a bad time. He knows better now. ☐ "Things change," says the twenty-four-year-old millworker. Marrying and having children thrust a bit of responsibility on him, but at some point Packy got scared, too. "All the deaths around here, wrecks and shootings—we were losing a lot of our Indian people. We still are. I've lost some pretty good friends." The way Packy figured it, even if he were lucky enough to avoid a calamity, he'd probably end up in and out of jail like his brothers. It was time to straighten out. ☐ For a few years now he's been turning down his old drinking buddies when they offer him beers. "They get mad but they get over it," says the guy whose nickname is "Kushume," Sahaptin for "bratty, crazy." Keeping busy seems to be the key. On the green chain at the mill, Packy pulls and stacks veneer all day; then he comes home to three kids under the age of two. When the salmon and steelhead come up the Deschutes River, Packy and his net are likely to be waiting for them on the family scaffold at Sherars Bridge. And during powwows his lungs get a workout in his brother's drumming and singing group. ☐ There's not much Packy feels he can do for his wayward contemporaries. "I just let 'em do what they want to do." But his kids are another matter. "I hope they have a better life than I had." When I asked Packy what kind of parent he felt he was, his ten-month-old boy—just rescued by his father from an overturned walker—suddenly flashed him an adoring, utterly contented smile. Packy smiled back and said nothing.

PACKY HEATH

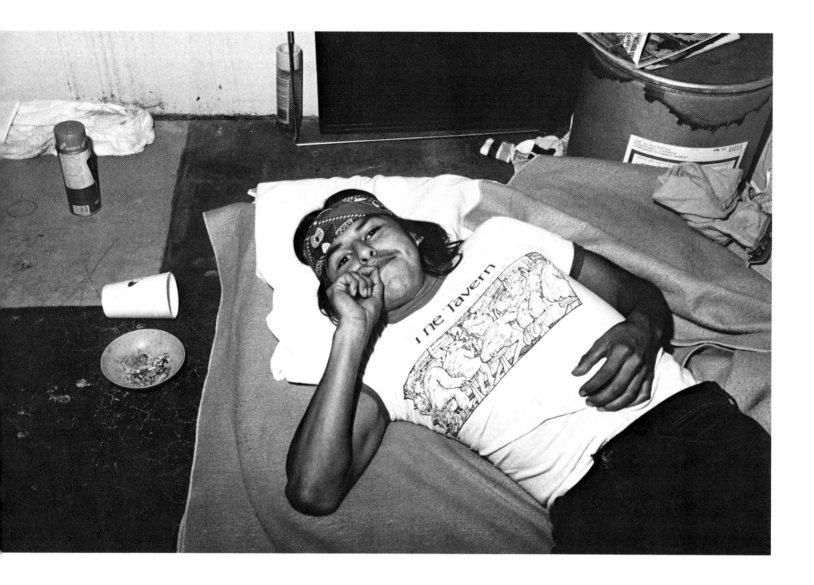

1981

IT'S HARD FOR LUCINDA to understand the young people of the reservation who aren't as tough as she was. It's even hard for her to accept her own frailties, as when she caught pneumonia while riding on the Tribes' float in Portland's Grand Floral Parade. For Lucinda—lean and big-boned—self-reliance has always been a virtue. ☐ "These young people, they're screwing up now," she insisted one day in her husky voice. "They go drinking all the time. It's not very good like that. I tells the girls, 'Now you run around, run around, chase boys and have a little baby!' They think they're smart but they ain't." ☐ Her own eight children were "good workers" on the family ranch at Sidwalter and she is proud of her thirty-six grandchildren. But Lucinda thinks all the reservation kids would be a lot better off if they'd grown up as she had. "I *had* to go to school," she said, although she didn't start until she was eleven and then went only through the fifth grade. Lucinda feels indebted to the much-maligned Warm Springs boarding school for its rigorous lessons in homemaking. "We were kitchen girls," she recalled. "Some of us made bread in big tubs. We had to get up at six o'clock in the morning and knead it down. We made everything. We had our own chickens and eggs. We made our own uniforms and did our own wash. We had orchards with apples and plums and peaches, and we cut the potatoes so the boys could plant them." She remembers less well the academic lessons; she spoke only Wasco until she went to school, and then "I talked broken language, not too straight." ☐ As a young wife living with her husband Alfred along the Deschutes River, Lucinda put her boarding school skills to work with her own orchards and chickens, supplemented by ducks and trout from the river and rabbits caught on the way back from market in Madras. From her grandmother, Lucinda had learned to gather and prepare Indian foods, too. "We never worked. We had plenty to eat. And we never took rations," she said proudly. Even today she shuns the twice-weekly senior citizen lunches at the center two doors away. Besides, "there's nobody there to talk Wasco with," she said. ☐ Perhaps if the young people understood Wasco, Lucinda could find just the right words to guide them. But anyone who is really looking will find an eloquent message in her stubborn jaw, her bright eyes. ☐ *Postscript: Lucinda's body gave out and she died in 1986 at the age of eighty-five.*

LUCINDA SMITH

1979

WITH TOBACCO TUCKED UNDER HER LIP, Ruthy talked about her young motherhood. On the Fourth of July after her sophomore year in high school, she went to watch fireworks with her boyfriend and didn't come home. "In Portland there were recreation centers and movies . . . it was a bigger space to run around," she recalled. "It was a dumb reason to take off. I wasn't having any problems at home—it just seemed like fun." She got pregnant while she was away and her sixteen-year-old sister, also pregnant and a runaway, looked after her. Ruthy came home to have Tony the next spring. Tony's father didn't stick around. A few months later, the teenage mother ran into Vernon, a childhood friend, at the Pi-Ume-Sha powwow and they rode around and talked. Soon Ruthy was pregnant again, but it was different this time—Vernon was asking her to marry him. □ "I warned him of all the responsibilities, taking care of Tony and the one coming," Ruthy recalled. "We talked about money, too, and about getting our own place." They married in October and moved in with Vernon's mother. Vernon tried to stay in school and play football, but he felt he should be the one bringing home the money so he quit in his senior year to get a job at the mill. Ruthy managed to earn her GED between having Gerald and Vernon, Jr. and dreamed of a job in data processing. □ The young couple didn't make it. Tony is with Ruthy's mom and Ruthy is trying to gain custody of the three youngest. She's going to court-ordered counseling and parenting classes, not because she feels they're useful but because she'll do whatever she has to do to get the kids back. "If I didn't think I could take care of my kids, I wouldn't have had them," she asserted, adding, "If I'm old enough to be pregnant, then I'm old enough to take care of them." □ Ruthy has no regrets about mothering at such a young age. "I love kids," she said with a big smile. "They take the place of running around. When I'm upset they'll do something that makes me laugh, then I forget about my problems. The best part is when they get older and call you Mom for the first time. They come in with a scratch and you can comfort them. I like being needed." □ *Postscript: At twenty-four, Ruthy put her reproductive days behind her. "Four is enough," she told me as she headed for her job in the Tribal Council office.*

STEVEN & TONY TIAS, RUTHY ANDERSON

1982

"ALL MY CHILDREN are so individual. No two are alike," says Bernice, longhouse elder, Head Start teacher, councilwoman, and eleven-times mother. "Their father [Art] never did fight with me and he's always been a good provider. If that's all the kids can be, that's good enough." ☐ Gloria *(fourth from right)*: "We sent her off to ballet school in Portland and she was just about to study under Maria Tallchief when she came home to play softball and popped her knee out." ☐ Jackson ("Big Oh" or "Butter") *(not pictured)*: "When I had Jackson, I think that's when my life of fear started. He used to have convulsions for a long time after we wrecked the car and I never knew how long we'd have him with us." ☐ Isaac *(not pictured)*: "He was just an in-between child you kind of forgets. Quiet, kind of timid." ☐ Aaron *(picture on mantle)*: Aaron brought the white and Indian kids together. When we lost him, it was quite a loss to both the Madras and Warm Springs communities." ☐ Nadine *(not pictured)*: "Nadine was one of the first day-care children here. She was quiet at first, but then she got meaner and meaner. I took her out of day-care. It made her insecure." ☐ Anthony ("Chaz") *(third from left)*: Tony was the pass-around boy. He was mad at me, mad at Art, and mad at the world. He drunk real heavy right after high school but then he married Robin, had two kids, and went to Serenity Lane." ☐ Rodney *(third from right)*: "Rodney got caught in the middle. He's real quiet, but he's my boy. When he comes home from college, he mops the floor and cleans up before he leaves." ☐ Eric ("Max") *(not pictured)*: "He was his grandmother's boy and he learned a lot of traditional things from her. Now he cuts wood and takes it to the old people. When you get children who have feelings for people, then you've done one good traditional thing." ☐ Elfreda ("Gilly") *(left foreground)*: "She always liked Indian dancing and beadwork. She thought because I did it, it was the way of life. One day she might be a good leader." ☐ Robinson ("Gorky") *(not pictured)*: "You'd want all your children to be like Gorky. He was a day-care child, too, a hand-me-down kid, but he loved to be happy and to make people happy. He was the dental poster boy for two years, but then his teeth fell out." ☐ Tonya *(right)*: "She's been spoiled from the beginning of time. Her brothers wanted her to be a tomboy and she could tackle most of the neighbor boys. ☐ *Postscript: Jackson died in another car wreck in 1985. Gilly named her new baby after him.*

74   BERNICE MITCHELL & FAMILY

1983

ON A WINTER AFTERNOON a couple of years after Annie's one hundredth birthday party, I drank coffee in the kitchen of the Dry Hollow homestead and listened to two of her children talk about their late mother. The summer before, another of her thirteen children had reminisced over a dish of huckleberries. ☐ Like any other mother remembered, Annie was pure, self-sacrificing, firm but kind, all-knowing, hard-working, and she baked the best pies. But Annie's kids, who admit that their self-described orneriness had to come from somewhere, also remember the woman who hollered at them in Wasco, flipped them with wet dish towels, packed a .38 pistol, and snuck an occasional cigarette from her cornhusk bag. ☐ The routine of life without electricity or running water lingers foremost in the family's mind. "That poor lady, she worked her head off for us," said Catherine. Images are conjured of Annie churning butter, canning fruits and garden vegetables, and cooking at her huge wood stove; butchering and drying salmon on the bank of the Columbia River; scrubbing the laundry on the rocks in Seekseequa Creek; doing beadwork, tanning deer hides and making moccasins and gloves to trade for barrels of flour, sugar, beans, and rice; sewing patches on top of patches on the family clothes; horseback riding *quinepuch* (double) with the smallest child up to the huckleberry patches; and even rounding up cattle and mending fences with her husband Wesley. ☐ There were the more private moments, too, as when newlywed Catherine didn't want to go up to her husband's bed. "I know it will hurt, but it's something you got to go through when you get married," Annie had advised. "Maybe you'll have children and that'll be nice." ☐ Getting old was Annie's biggest challenge. "She didn't like to be helpless," said Zelma, the youngest, who lived with Annie all her life. "When she couldn't get up and do things herself, that's the first time I ever saw her cry." ☐ There had never been enough time in Annie's life to cultivate self-pity, and old age was no excuse to start. Alvis likes to tell about the day he was easing his mother down the front steps in her wheelchair, when he lost his hold and the chair went bumping and careening down the remaining steps. At the end of the ride, Annie was slumped down in the chair, her scarf hanging rakishly to one side. She looked up at Alvis, smiled, and said, "If I wasn't a damn tough cowgirl, I wouldn't have made it!"

1982

OPENING THE DOOR of her family's trailer on Sidwalter Flat, C.R. carries a coiled rope in her hand. In the middle of the living room, a wooden "steer" offers its horns for practice throws. The 1984 barrel-racing champion of the Western States Indian Rodeo Association is an up-and-coming roper. ☐ Through the 1970s, the name "Squiemphen" was synonymous with barrel-racing, as all five of Earl and Rita's girls competed in the traditional women's rodeo event. While each sister dropped out, C.R. kept on—and kept on winning. "There's a lot of things I've wanted to do, but about the only thing I've really stuck with is rodeo, roping, and horses," she says. And while one hand collects prize money for barrel-racing, the other hand slowly toughens from the burning and bone-crunching rope. ☐ During hours of practice in her uncle's corral, C.R. "heads" and her sister Sammi "heels"; but when it comes to competing, C.R. teams up with men. The rodeo world (where rest rooms are labeled "barrel-racers and "bronc riders") isn't ready for all-woman roping. "When I first started roping," says C.R., "the men laughed. They thought I was just a dumb girl and should stick with barrel-racing. Now, at least in Warm Springs, I'm just kind of one of the guys." ☐ So it is in her family. Terry, the single Squiemphen boy, kept hoping for a brother but finally decided to make boys of his younger sisters—an easy enough task on a cattle ranch. Eventually Terry, a bronc rider, pressed the girls into rodeoing. It was an immediate obsession for C.R., who came to feel like a "square peg" when away from her rodeo family or the rodeo arena. She managed to finish high school (she wore a big, black cowboy hat for her senior picture), but college plans were temporarily eclipsed when she started making payments on a new horse trailer and diesel pickup. Her social life has revolved around the rodeo circuit and the only job she's found that comes close to the excitement of rodeoing is fighting forest and range fires. ☐ There have been times when the cowgirl luster has worn off a bit for C.R., but something always happens: her professional women's rodeo permit arrives in the mail, she wins her first saddle, or she qualifies again for the Indian National Finals. Nothing can match the adrenalin that flows when C.R. and her family roll into new rodeo grounds with their trailer in tow; unless it's the peace she feels when she's working her horses on the windswept plain that has always been her home.

C.R. SQUIEMPHEN

1986

WHEN YOU LOVE TO RODEO, you can't quit," says Jazzie, reriding a memorable bucking horse between beers at Cliff's Tavern, a popular watering hole at Pine Grove where "you can sell out without getting throwed out." Morphine, horse linament, and DMSO have kept him in the arena despite broken ankles, severed fingers, and crushed legs. His girlfriend still can't get him to quit. It's always "one more go-around" for the fifty-two-year-old cowboy. □ "At first it just meant a lot of fun. Then it was like a part-time job. Now jobs are hard to get around here, so I hit the rodeos pretty hard and try to win as much money as I can." Jazzie's been winning about three thousand dollars a season, not counting a wealth of silver buckles, spurs, and tack. Rodeoing often precludes holding a regular job. Monday morning comes and goes and a cowboy might still be on the road after a rodeo a thousand miles away. "And there's always someone offering 'just one more drink.' If it's an Indian show, I can't make it back. If it's a professional show, I can't make it back." □ A timber faller and bull buck in the reservations's forest for years, Jazzie is now gambling on his prowess as a mugger in the wild horse race event. "Stout, strong-armed and crazy," Jazzie earned the national title of "Best Wild Horse Mugger" in 1979 and claimed a spot in the National Cowboy Hall of Fame, all for his finesse in twisting and biting wild horses' ears so teammates can saddle and ride the unwilling beasts. □ "It's been a long, deadly trail I've been down," admits Jazzie. "I don't know where it'll go." But Jazzie's old friends—his boots, his buckles, and a can of beer—will likely be with him at trail's end.

1982

WHEN RADIO CAME to the reservation, Kenman was ready. "I listen to tunes all night, man. Might as well get paid for it!" he said after applying for a spot at KWSI. With jive on his tongue and music in his blood, Kenman had always seemed like a deejay without a studio. ☐ His midnight-to-six listeners liked him right away. He spoke their language, his mellow delivery laced with local slang. He planned "soul hour" for the two A.M. slot to help tavern denizens get home safely after closing time. It was pure, unadulterated Kenman from the start. ☐ "This job is just right up my alley," he says. "I've always been a music man." His earliest musical memories, other than what he heard in the longhouse and at powwows, were of Elvis Presley, The Platters, and Anthony and the Imperials. A 1966 snapshot of Kenman in the family album shows a skinny teenager with black-rimmed glasses, pegged pants, white socks, and a cigarette—Buddy Holly gone "skin." The aspiring musician collected an assortment of guitars and drums and used to "jam all day" by himself or with his brothers and friends, occasionally sitting in on the congas with a professional band. "Music is pretty much my life. It's everybody's life, init? I can't think of anybody who doesn't hum, whistle, sing, or something. Nobody can say they don't like music." ☐ Kenman likes delivering it. Working in the woods was the only other job that gave him the same satisfaction; now in the pre-dawn hours when his old crew buddies are heading out to the woods, the deejay reminds them to take along their water. Being the mailman for the tribal offices had been okay for flirting and making dates with secretaries. The green chain at the mill was a drag. So were the dry periods in between jobs—when beer, Indian ball, and his tunes were his steadfast companions. And it's hard for Kenman to talk charitably about the four years he spent in the Navy watching bombs light up the Vietnam night. ☐ Now the night is his. In the KWSI studio, equipped with endless coffee, scores of tape cartridges, and a hundred thousand watts of power, Kenman makes a living being himself.

KEN "KENMAN" MILLER

□ 1986

THERE IS ALWAYS a faint smile on Sammy's face when he's matching wits with a reservation tree. Looking the tree up and down, he notes the lay of the land and yanks the starter on his chainsaw. His smile intensifies as the saw chews a wedge out of the trunk and he circles the tree to make the undercut. The wood creaks and pops and sends the grinning cutter running. "I just like to cut logs," says Sammy after the tree has thundered to the forest floor. "It's all I've ever done and all I want to do." ☐ It's all Sammy has been doing since 1949, when a logger lured him away from the pumps at the Warm Springs service station and into the woods of Oregon and Washington. He had spent part of the war in an internment camp with his Japanese father and Wasco mother, then spent the rest of it fighting in the Pacific. He briefly considered a military career, but then came home with no plans. Falling timber sounded okay to Sammy. ☐ He and a partner started their own business on the reservation in 1965, and in the first month Sammy netted sixty-four dollars, "not even enough to make a car payment." But business picked up and Sammy has made a good living from the woods, enough to provide for eight step-children and satisfy his love for the racetrack. He recently had to trim his crew of fifteen fallers down to seven, and "the way the market is going, I'm thinking of cutting that down, too. It's a rat race out there. The mill cuts us back in the beginning of the season, and expects us to make it up. Then the weather gets bad." ☐ Like many loggers and fallers on the reservation, Sammy keeps to himself. "I rarely go to Warm Springs—just to get the mail. I don't mix much with the people here—I'm always afraid I'll say the wrong thing. But I'm proud of my Indian blood, no one can deny me that." ☐ Sammy puts out his cigarette, wipes the sawdust off his glasses, and shoulders his saw. He ambles down the length of his fallen log, a tape measure snaking out behind him. He's a little slower now, but the "brush" is still the place for him.

SAMMY DANZUKA

1981

W ILSON'S MY MIDDLE NAME. Born on the day Woodrow Wilson was inaugurated, I'll be sixty-two tomorrow—I hope the next sixty-two years are easier." Woody's words come out in the staccato style of a stand-up comedian, a cigar always wagging in his mouth. But Woody is frequently dead serious. District commander of the local VFW, judge of the tribal election board, vice chairman of the law-and-order committee, deputy sheriff, and ex-police chief, Woodrow Wilson Smith seems to have been born to serve his community and his country. ☐ Woody retired from log truck driving in 1967 with a one hundred percent disability, suffering the delayed effects of a concussion received from a German 88 blast in France during the Second World War. Woody was proud to have been a "foot slogger" on behalf of his country, and in 1952 he helped found the nation's first all-Indian VFW post. ☐ Across the street from the VFW Hall in Warm Springs is the old teen center, which now serves as the voting hall. Woody and his wife Iris have spent many long election days greeting voters there, followed by long nights counting votes. Woody interprets the ballots for old folks, listens to gripes, and occasionally sheds some light on the issue being considered. Sometimes when he reports the election results to Tribal Council, he tells them that the people aren't as informed as they should be. "But it's hard for a layman like me to make recommendations," says Woody. ☐ It's hard just *being* a layman for Woody, especially when it comes to law enforcement. There is only the hint of humor when he suggests he is still the chief of police because of a disagreement over the terms under which he left the department in 1963. But now the glory of refusing bribes from speeding motorists and the anguish of "pulling mangled kids out of wrecks" belongs to others. Woody still has a hand in police affairs through the law-and-order committee, but for action he must be content to listen to his scanner twenty-four hours a day, display his deputy's badge, and target shoot with his twenty rifles and six pistols. A full-time citizen like Woody is never completely off-duty. ☐ *Postscript: Woody came out of retirement to serve as the interim chief judge for the Tribal Court during 1984. The VFW Hall was razed the same year and the voting hall is now a sporting goods store.*

WOODY SMITH

1979

HE RAN A STRING OF TAXIS in Honolulu and owned nightclubs around Oregon before coming back to the reservation in 1980 to go into business with his brother Mickey. He didn't know anything about rock crushing, but soon he was "making big rocks into small ones and cleaning them" for a half dozen accounts on the reservation. Ted feels good about keeping dollars in the community, a cause the Tribal Council chose to back when it leased the land to Ted. ☐ Fellow Wascos are apt to think he is progressive. Others might feel he's taken on the way of the white man. Ted says he's just making a living the way he knows best—as his own boss. "It's not just the money," he says of his ambitions. "It's being a member of the Confederated Tribes, accomplishing the things you set out to do, and feeling like what you do benefits the Tribes as a whole." ☐ Ted is proud of his Wasco heritage. Before the treaty, he recounts, the Wascos were the "standard-bearers" for the Northwest tribes and they wielded social and economic influence that won the respect of Indians and white men alike. Ted's own grandfather, Judge Jerry Brunoe, made a lasting impression on him with his repeated advice to learn to get along with all kinds of people. ☐ During his off-hours, the entrepreneur likes to ponder scenarios for his own and the Tribes' future. Financial success starts with education, he insists, education that "teaches the importance of retaining cultural values while developing the natural resources." So why not establish a community college in Warm Springs? To enhance tribal assets, why not build a ski resort on Mt. Jefferson? While he waits for such developments, Ted reads all the literature on Columbia River history that he can get his hands on. He is jotting down notes for a book about his ancestors, its theme resonating in his head: "I know where I've been, but I wonder where I'm going."

TED BRUNOE

1981

WARM SPRINGS CHEVRON is a family, with the many moods of a family. Gas pumps and hydraulic lifts have been the backdrop for a decade full of Clements family dramas. But any clouds gathering on George or Janice's brow usually clear when a customer rolls up. They like seeing their friends and relatives come through and they get a kick out of the tourists. ☐ They've stuck with it through unpaid credit, bad checks, and a shrinking profit margin. It was easier when Janice's brother Robert was alive; of the three partners, Robert had the brains, says Janice. But he died in a house fire in 1975 and took some of the spirit of the venture with him. Since then, George and Janice have survived two nationwide gas shortages, spiraling gas prices, and competition from an independent dealer down the road. Now there is competition from their landlord, the Tribes. "At first, they and the BIA gave me a lot of business," said George. "Their rigs gassed up here and brought in about $500 to $700 a month. Then they built the motor pool and a $400,000 tribal garage that's open on weekends now, and they won't spend a cent on this building. They say I'm mismanaging the business. I don't know; I feel kind of let down." ☐ The new tribal garage is a symbol for George. A champion of youth programs, particularly since his oldest son was shot and killed at a party in the family home in 1977, George has challenged tribal priorities that seem to ensure better service for cars than for kids. "It's the tribal managers' job to make money for the Tribes, but it's the Tribal Council's job to keep them in tow, to be sensitive to what the members need." ☐ George and Janice do what they can. They have served on the law-and-order and health-and-welfare committees, they are outspoken at general council meetings, they open their home (and station) to foster kids, neighbor kids, and grandkids. The bills get paid, partly with a Christmas tree business that George and his three brothers operate on tribal land. But if a sigh is heard while the gas is being pumped at the station, it's because running a business and raising a family are two of the most difficult jobs in Warm Springs. ☐ *Postscript: Janice challenged the tribal budget with a petition in 1985 and was elected to Tribal Council in 1986.*

GEORGE & JANICE CLEMENTS

1981

MOTHER'S DAY, 1982. Dad is watching afternoon wrestling on television. Robert Jr., six months, sleeps in a tiny hammock strung across the living room. Sadie, two, and Elsie, one, both in underwear, squabble over toys and take turns sipping Dad's tall KoolAid. Foster son Leon, eleven, in pajamas, and Tracy, six, rescue the roll of toilet paper Elsie has stretched the length of the hall. Mother, twenty-three, emerges from the shower, her long hair wrapped in a towel. ☐ Marella became a mother at seventeen, married her boyfriend Robert a couple of years later and had three more babies in quick succession. "I wish I would have finished school," she says in retrospect, "but I really like having these guys." She controls the chaos in various ways. "I puts them down to nap when my soap operas are on," she explains. "And at powwows—my step-father thinks this is terrible—I puts harnesses on them and ties them to a tepee. One time we lost Sadie at Pendleton. We all went crazy." ☐ One of Marella's pressure valves is her own mother, who cared for Tracy during his first year until the young mother was ready. Now Marella can drop off her kids with her mom or an aunt when she wants to go for a ride with Robert or party with friends. When Robert's mill salary runs short, Marella's mom helps out with money for Pampers. Marella herself bailed out a single mother of five by taking in Leon—a frequent guest who finally found a legal home with the Sams. ☐ Slowly the family gets dressed in preparation for a Mother's Day dinner at Grandma's. They will celebrate motherhood, entered into so casually, shared with the community so freely, and revered above all other institutions on the reservation. Marella's mother taught her, and Marella is teaching her own daughters, to be a Warm Springs mother. ☐ *Postscript: "We've got little Neda now—she's twenty months," said Marella in 1986. Leon went back to his natural mother.*

1981

I'M EVERYBODY'S GRANDMA!" laughs Susan, whose nickname is a child's way of saying *katla*, the Sahaptin word for mother's mother. ☐ Kussa has a tribally built senior citizen's house in Simnasho, but she prefers to stay at the homes of her many children and grandchildren. There is one home she yearns to live in again—a big weathered house on the bench above Warm Springs. I photographed her there, at the big house she had lived in for twenty years, abandoned a few years before as if someone had gone out for groceries and had never come back. Snapshots were wedged into mirror frames, bedding lay rumpled on mattresses, and a piano sat tuneless in the rear entryway. She looked at the vines curling through the windows, the mouse droppings in the corners, and the holes in the roof that let in both starlight and rain, and she was sad. When she stepped out onto the back stoop and gazed at the hills, she thought of other times and other houses. ☐ Her first home was a "wigwam" with a dirt floor. "*Every*body was poor then," she said. "Some of these people, they say 'we had this' or 'we had that,' but no-o-o. I'm telling the truth. Nobody had anything!" Kussa remembers patching and repatching moccasins and wearing gunnysacks for overshoes. She and her neighbors got through the winters by trading dried Indian foods and hand-sewn buckskin gloves, worth a dollar a pair, for the sugar, coffee, and other new foods they'd come to depend on. It hadn't been easy ever since "those people came over the ocean and followed their sheep" into her people's lands. ☐ Susan and her husband Bill had farmed and kept cattle and horses near Simnasho, and after living for years in a breezy, rough lumber house, they graduated to a surplus Army barrack. When Bill's pickup flipped over and killed him on the Simnasho grade in 1953 Kussa reluctantly left the farm and moved into the big house at Warm Springs. ☐ It was her daughter Adeline's house, built by her husband's family in 1927, but Kussa soon began to think of it as her own. It was the nicest house she'd lived in, and she tried to keep up with the repairs, letting the bills fall to her daughter. But Adeline ran out of loan money, and one winter day when the pipes froze, the family moved out. ☐ Adeline has a new home next door to the big house. One of Kussa's grandsons lives on the other side. And when Kussa stays with them, she tries not to notice the vines growing longer, the holes getting bigger.

SUSAN "KUSSA" MOSES

1979

ERLAND EMBARRASSED SALLY by coming to her natural childbirth classes, but he knew even before Ambrosia was born that he wanted to be an involved father. When he brought Sally, a Yakima, back to the reservation to have the baby, it signaled the end of his wandering. ☐ They moved in with Erland's mother, whose house had as many as twenty people coming and going at one time. Erland found temporary work while he waited for his name to come up on the mill waiting list, and they were able to move into a new tribal duplex. There I visited them, interested in this new family I kept encountering around the the community—at quilt classes, swim-baby lessons, my own photography class, and the store. They formed a unit that looked gentle and intentional, not haphazard like many of their contemporaries. ☐ Sally and Erland sat on a large cushion on the living room floor, bouncing Ambrosia, while powwow music pulsated from the stereo. Relatives drinking beer at the dining room table got noisier. We shouted our conversation, with occasional echoes and comments from the other room. I asked the couple what values they planned to teach Ambrosia. Sally deferred to Erland, saying, "That's his job," but adding, "I just want her to have a better life than I've had." Erland, whose own childhood was filled with Boy Scouts, good grades, and traditional teachings, said simply, "I guess she'll just learn from watching us." Ambrosia, wide-eyed, looked around her world curiously. ☐ *Postscript: In the spring of 1986, Erland was working the planer chain at the mill and the couple was selecting a four-bedroom house plan for their land on Schoolie Flat. Ambrosia was talking about having a horse and a cow and a baby sister.*

1982

AROUND THE GOLF COURSE, Zane's nickname is "Chairman" and he's known for his high wagers in the "horse race" event and for periodic flashes of temper when his ball sails into the rough. In the Tribal Council chambers, the two-term chairman is known for his careful, even-handed leadership. ☐ Zane and I got along better on the golf course, where I shot more pictures and asked fewer questions. He and his fellow councilmen were skilled at dodging reporters' queries, and during a particularly sensitive year of budget discussions the Council seemed to go into executive session whenever they saw me coming. It was only after I'd left *Spilyay Tymoo* that Zane relaxed and opened up to me. There was a reason why its individual members offered "no comment," he said. It was a matter of tradition. ☐ "A lot of good-thinking people got us to where we are now," Zane told me. "People with limited knowledge of the English language were able to get terms put in the treaty that turned out to be invaluable. And all through the years, our leaders have negotiated the settlement of issues instead of going to court. As a result, we've gained the respect of some of our neighboring governments." The process may seem painfully slow at times, but the tradition at work is consensus. "The three different tribes are able to forget their tribal backgrounds and work together for the benefit of the Confederated Tribes," said Zane. ☐ Zane's father Charlie, a cattleman with little education and a lot of insight, was a councilman from the 1930s to the 1960s, a time when some of the reservation's most important decision-making was occurring. Zane grew up surrounded by his father's philosophy of leadership. "Use your common sense and you'll figure it out" was one tenet, along with "Don't rush into anything—consider everything" and "Get along with the white man—he's here to stay." ☐ Shying away from a political life, Zane built up his seniority at the mill while his brother Vernon added education to common sense and became the Tribes' first general manager. By 1971, Charlie had retired and Vernon had died, and Zane—then a successful independent logger—decided he was ready to carry on where his family had left off. ☐ From behind mountains of papers on the contemporary oak Council table, Zane and ten others gently take the reservation from their ancestors and deliver it to their children.

ZANE JACKSON

1983

DOWN IN THE BATCH PLANT, where Jim was making sure the concrete was up to specs, the young inspector trainee didn't realize the foundation for a career was being laid along with the critical footings for the Tribes' new hydroelectric project. As Jim remembers it, "Finally it dawned on me, hey, I could be working into something here!" ☐ Now Jim is the assistant project manager ("make sure you say 'trainee'," he insists) of the first federally licensed hydroelectric facility owned by an American Indian tribe. Jim listens to the steady roar of the turbine, watches the many gauges and signal lights, and sees that maintenance is done properly at the mostly automated plant, which converts the flow of the Deschutes River into eight million kilowatts of electricity in the average month. ☐ "I know how it works and how to fix it, but I want to know the theory," says Jim, who has learned all he knows about engineering from people on the job. "If I'd had my act together after high school, I'd have been out of college at the time the project went on-line." Now, Jim faces five years of engineering school or some specialized training before the "trainee" can be dropped from his title. ☐ The son of a tribal member and a non-Indian tribal manager, Jim was raised to expect a lot of himself. "I didn't feel I was any better than anyone else, but I wanted to be a self-made type of guy—a manager like my dad, or a businessman. I wanted to do something different—something the community needed but didn't have." ☐ Tribal Council had an idea of what was needed. "They wanted a tribal member running this project one day and they've encouraged me the whole way," says Jim. This kind of foresight has characterized the project right from the start, Jim feels. He admires the generation of tribal leaders who slipped a few words into the 1955 Pelton Dam contract with Portland General Electric that allowed a tribal turbine to be installed in the PGE reregulating dam. "They were so unselfish," says Jim. "They made long-term decisions that had no immediate benefit for them." ☐ Now Jim, at twenty-four, feels some of the weight of the reservation's future resting on him. "It makes you wonder," he says, "if you're making the right decisions for your kids and your kids' kids."

JIM MANION

1984

YOU CAN CALL THIS 'Silhouette of a Fading Era,'" said Olney Patt, Sr. as I photographed him leaning on the corral at the Patt Ranch near Indian Head Canyon. He was watching his kids and grandkids brand, castrate, and tag the ears of the North End's new crop of calves. "It's hard to be on the outside of the corral looking in," he added later. "You just reminisce about how it used to be done." ☐ In the same way, Olney looks back at nearly thirty years on the Tribal Council. A wily politician who always knew the right time and the right way to talk to his people, Olney operated according to his grandfather's credo: "Always reserve something for the future generations." With that in mind, the young rancher picked the hay out of his clothes, overcame his fear of airplanes, made friends with Oregon's congressional delegation, and teamed up with the Tribes' attorney Owen Panner for three decades of high political drama. ☐ He was there in the Senate gallery when a century-old reservation boundary dispute was being settled with the passage of the McQuinn Act. He was there at the longhouse when his people were struggling with the question of distributing or banking the four million dollar settlement from the Army Corps of Engineers for the Celilo fishing grounds. He was up until 2:30 A.M. negotiating with officers of First National Bank of Oregon when the Tribes were seeking a loan to purchase the sawmill. And Olney wasn't just a witness to such critical moments. He was in the thick of them, presenting a key compromise, a fresh way of looking at things, or just a certain eloquence that would nudge the issue toward resolution. ☐ Ever since he was a teenager at Chemawa Indian School in Salem and heard Commissioner of Indian Affairs John Collier speak about the new 1934 Indian Reorganization Act, Olney had had a vision. Fascinated with the idea of the act's revolving credit programs, Olney began scheming. "We could have better homes, better farm equipment," he remembered thinking. "We'd be able to set up our own mill and process our own timber. We'd have our own police force and tribal court. I could see a better tomorrow for our Tribes." It remained for him to go home and convince fellow tribal members. He was becoming a politician. ☐ Now the tribes have everything he dreamed about. Still a councilman, Olney prefers the days when "we had to fight every inch. Today, politics are more professional than they were in my time. There's very little of that 'Indian touch' anymore." So, the man who helped establish the herd is now standing outside the corral, watching the dust fly around a new generation of cattlemen.

1985

HAND INTO STONE

Her creped fingers,
teethmarked with red speckles,
held mine tight
as she showed our finger moons to me.
They grew together as snowy stones
scratching themselves sleepily.

She had long fingers
with the mobility of spiders.
I felt them at night
as they climbed my skin.
She wrapped us
in tight shells
with agate crystals.

We breathed our own breath
under this cover.

—Elizabeth Woody

1986

THE RESERVATION

TWO CRISES SURVIVED

O N A JUNE DAY in 1855, fifty years after Lewis and Clark had exchanged friendly greetings with the Indians of the mid-Columbia River, a small group of tribal headmen, government men, and interpreters smoked together at the river village of Wasco in the Oregon Territory. Superintendent of Indian Affairs Joel Palmer was polite but persistent. "We have found that the white man and Indian cannot long live together in peace, that it is better that lines should be drawn," he said.   Two days later, Kuck-up of the Upper Deschutes band was convinced. "We do not wish to have our garden joining to the white man's. I wish now to do as you have said, to live aside from the whites." ☐ The land General Palmer offered on behalf of the U. S. Government was only somewhat familiar to the people who had roamed from river to mountains to grasslands for thousands of years. They had their favorite haunts—the gentle Tygh Valley, the rocky root fields east of the Deschutes River, and the life-sustaining Columbia—for which they argued eloquently. About the proposed piece of land, Mark, headman of the Wascos said, "The place you have mentioned, I have not seen. There is no Indians or whites there yet, and that is the reason I say I know nothing about that country. If there were whites and Indians there then I would think it was a good country." But Palmer was in a hurry, the papers had already been drawn up, and it became a point of honor for the delegates to oblige the government man more quickly than had the Cayuses during similar negotiations a few days before. ☐ Reluctantly, 151 of the assembled tribal representatives signed their x-marks to a treaty that ceded millions of acres to the U. S. Government for one hundred fifty thousand dol-

108

Traditional dip-net fishing was common at Celilo Falls on the Columbia River into the 1950s, but was ended when The Dalles Dam flooded the ancient sites in 1957. (OHS neg. 65996)

lars in goods and services, and reserved a 578,000-acre corner of their homeland for the exclusive use of their people. Thus was born the Warm Springs Indian Reservation.

Although the Treaty of 1855 was not ratified by Congress until 1859, the move to the reservation be-

gan the year after the treaty council at Wasco. Concerned for the welfare of their elders, women, and children, and lured by such treaty promises as education, privacy, and continued access to off-reservation hunting, fishing, and gathering sites, tribal leaders packed up their people and moved south. But the dis-

placed people soon learned that the government was slow to come through on promises and that farmers' fences spoke louder than treaty rights. Poverty became all too familiar to a people whose traditional way of life had kept them well-fed and not wanting.

Today, any bitterness that survives from that uprooting is overshadowed by a profound pride in the reservation and the treaty that created it. The outline of the reservation can be seen on flags, T-shirts, and beaded items, and a powwow commemorates the Treaty of 1855. That adopted piece of ground bounded by two rivers and two mountain ranges has become a source of strength and unity for a still distinct people. The river tribes had been effectively removed from the path of white settlers, but they did not languish in their isolation. Instead, they found use for their timbered acreage and fast-flowing streams and learned to use the treaty's protections to their advantage. A solemn day in 1855 produced a piece of paper and a piece of land that today are springboards for a resourceful people.

One hundred years later, another drama unfolded along the Columbia River. People from the Warm Springs, Yakima, and Umatilla reservations stood on the bluffs overlooking Celilo Falls and watched the waters rise until their fishing grounds were swallowed up in silence. The closing of the gates at The Dalles Dam had ended thousands of years of continuous human history at the site, transforming the rocky precipices and roaring channels of water into a placid lake, and destroying the livelihood of generations of fishermen.

The Columbia River was at the heart of Wasco and Sahaptin culture, offering up the salmon that was the core of their diet as well as a valued trade item. Even into the 1950s, reservation families camped at Celilo during the summer and dipped their nets from scaffolds that clung to the slippery rocks, pulling up tons of salmon and steelhead each day. When Celilo was inundated in 1957, it was far more than a cultural vestige that was lost. Many fishermen who had grown up along the river knew no other way to make a living and returned to the reservation with idle hands and little

hope. Families tried to satisfy their taste for salmon with store-bought food or rations. But most importantly, the community's whole seasonal rhythm was disrupted, not as dramatically as a century before, but more finally.

The tribes of the Columbia had been unable to withstand the pressures of a country clamoring for electricity and irrigation water, just as their ancestors had been unable to stop the tide of settlers. No amount of money could compensate the people for the cultural loss, but Warm Springs tribal leaders had no choice but to accept a four million dollar settlement from the U.S. Army Corps of Engineers. It remained for the Confederated Tribes of Warm Springs, by then a chartered corporation, to invest the money wisely and make the most of another setback.

And that they did. Rather than distributing the whole settlement among tribal members, most of the sum was deposited in the U. S. Treasury, to be held in trust for Warm Springs. The Tribes' first big expenditure was an Oregon State College (now University) study of the reservation's resources and their potential for economic development. Today, with a stable forest products industry, a luxury resort, a hydroelectric plant, and more jobs than people to fill them, the Tribes have made the Celilo money work for them beyond anyone's expectations. The flooding of the falls still hurts deeply, and the cultural damage can never be repaired, but the Tribes have endured.

They are survivors, these people of the river, as are the Paiutes who came later to the Warm Springs Reservation. They have had the wisdom to see the inevitability of the white culture's encroachments, the resilience to turn adversity to advantage, and the corporate strength to ride out the vagaries of federal Indian policy. The culture has suffered and individual lives have been sacrificed, but the Tribes have survived. It may be impossible to speculate about the future of the people of Warm Springs, but whatever course they take in the coming decades will be of their own shaping.

ANCIENT PEOPLE IN A NEW LAND

LEGEND TELLS OF a time when the earth's only "people" were animals, and Coyote came up the river to change them to humans. Traditional longhouse beliefs embrace a creation story much like Adam and Eve. Modern anthropology traces the origins of all North American natives to waves of Ice Age hunters following game across the Bering land bridge from Asia. The different explanations agree on one point: that the people's history goes back thousands of years. Ancestors of the people of Warm Springs are believed to have occupied what is now Oregon for at least 11,000 years, or 5,000 years before civilization began developing in Egypt. ☐ In a dry, steep-walled valley carved out of the earth by the powerful Columbia River, ancestors of today's Warm Springs and Wasco people learned the ways of the salmon and became expert fishermen and traders. To the south, in a vast basin of receding lakes and little rain, the Paiute people learned to survive with a spare, nomadic way of life. The brown skin and black hair of the river and basin people spoke of a single origin, but for thousands of years they evolved separately, their cultures finely tuned to their natural environments and their language and traditions quite distinct. ☐ They were strangers to each other, but not to the earth, which instilled the same rhythm in their cultures. Life for Oregon's first inhabitants moved in a circle with the seasons, a circle that for millennia went unchanged. Time was measured by the angle and intensity of the sun, the amount of moisture in the air or soil, the number of wrinkles on an old person's face, or the size of a pregnant woman's belly. At the center of the people's existence and their imagination was the earth, with its many moods, inhabitants, and forces. The

111

earth dictated a daily and seasonal regimen, and suggested a spiritual orientation for the people. The earth gave, the people gratefully received, and life had a natural balance and order that the people never tried to alter. Occasionally betrayed by volcanic eruptions, earthquakes, and floods, the people nevertheless maintained their allegiance to the earth.

It was the coming of a third, light-colored people that would change them forever. Then the cultures that seemed so durable would prove to be fragile, their delicate partnership with the natural world easily sundered. With their aboriginal homes giving way to the newcomers, the people of the river and the people of the desert basin would come to know each other through conflict. One day, they would find themselves sharing a square of land and a common destiny—as "Indians."

Lacking a written language, these early river and basin people left no historical records beyond the carved drawings that try to speak to us from rock walls. We learn what we can from arrow points, fire pits, and other archaeological remains. We listen to their descendants tell stories that are rich in symbolism but not in historical detail. We read the field notes of early explorers, flawed as they may be with haste and cultural bias. And we depend on a crop of anthropological studies from the 1930s, based on interviews with informants barely alive at the time of the treaty. Piecing it all together, we can begin to conjecture about life as it was before the coming of the whites.

LIFE ALONG THE GREAT RIVER

High on a basalt outcropping on the north side of the Columbia River, the petroglyph "Tsagiglalal" or "She Who Watches" has kept her eye on the villages below ever since Coyote decided there could be no more woman chiefs and changed her into rock. She was watching when U. S. explorers Meriwether Lewis and William Clark came down the river in the autumn of 1805. What she saw was a series of friendly encounters between the expedition members and her own people. What Lewis and Clark saw was recorded in great detail in their journals.

They described the people of the mid-Columbia as stocky and brown-skinned, with black hair worn long and loose, and pierced noses decorated with shells. The river people dressed minimally, in breechcloths, aprons, or short skin robes. Many, especially the women, had flattened heads, pressed in cradleboards during infancy to create a shape that was pleasing to them. The explorers noted some tumors, bad eyes, bad teeth, and swollen legs in evidence, but few if any signs of the venereal disease, smallpox, or other non-native diseases that already plagued American Indian tribes that had had direct and prolonged contact with whites. Lewis and Clark figured they were the first white people the mid-Columbia natives had ever seen.

The villagers, Lewis and Clark noted, were of "mild disposition and friendly disposed." That was fortunate for the explorers, who were getting short on supplies and had trading on their minds. In fact, Lewis and Clark had floated into the center of one of North America's largest aboriginal trade networks. They soon realized they were dealing with seasoned businesspersons who knew from their downriver neighbors what could be extracted from white people. As Clark observed in his journal, "They ask high prices for what they Sell and Say that the white people below give great prices for everything &c."

The expedition depended on the river people's knowledge of the Columbia and its idiosyncracies to guide them through the many treacherous rapids and narrows. At Celilo Falls the explorers' two guides from the upper Columbia said they wished to return to their bands, claiming not to be familiar with the language downriver and fearing hostilities from the people there. While Lewis and Clark found friendly people below the falls too, Celilo was a definite cultural dividing line.

From the upper reaches of *Nchi Wana**, or Great River, to just below Celilo Falls ranged the people who spoke dialects of the Sahaptin language and who shared a culture known today as "Plateau." Theirs was a sweeping, semi-arid region of volcanic deposits topped with grass, sagebrush, juniper, and cut with

---

* All Indian language words used here are in Sahaptin, unless otherwise noted.

The petroglyph Tsagiglalal, or She Who Watches, has kept an eye on the people of the Columbia in the vicinity of Celilo for as long as people can remember. (OHS neg. 52078)

canyons, a region of bitterly cold winters and blazingly hot summers. The Sahaptin-speakers whose descendants are the Warm Springs tribe lived in three principal groupings along the Columbia: the Tenino at a narrow place in the river above the present city of The Dalles; the Wyam just above Celilo Falls and near the mouth of the Deschutes River; and the John Day near the mouth of the John Day River. Their villages were usually in pairs, with secondary winter settlements removed from the windy Columbia. A fourth group, the Tygh, occupied sites well up the Deschutes River and in the nearby Tygh valley.

113

Without a single name for themselves, these bands of mid-Columbia natives were given various names by the whites, including Walla-Walla, as referred to in the treaty, and Tenino, after the Indians' name for their largest village (*Tinainu*). In pre-treaty discussion the author will call them Sahaptin, after their language.

Below Celilo and down to the eastern entrance of the Columbia River Gorge, lived a people whose language was not intelligible to the Sahaptins. These upper Chinook-speakers came to be called Wasco, after their principal village *Wasqu*, a Chinook word describing a cup-shaped rock and associated spring located near The Dalles. Along with the Wishram people on the north side of the river, the Wascos shared some of the social patterns and values of their downriver and coastal relatives, and their language was related to tongues spoken west of the Cascade Mountains.*

The river was at the center of both Wasco and Sahaptin cultures, but the Wascos, who lived by the river year-round, were more specialized as fishermen and traders. They were the dominating influence in the Columbia River trade network, and as such they were very conscious of wealth and status. Quite cosmopolitan, the Wascos spoke a trade language called "Chinook jargon," which enabled them to communicate with other tribes and eventually with Europeans. The Sahaptins were also highly skilled at fishing and trading, but perhaps because they were part of a much larger group of culturally and linguistically related peoples along the river, they were a little less open to other people, more self-contained. The blend of worldliness and parochialism at Warm Springs today is no doubt rooted in these traditional cultural differences.

The warm months were the busiest time of year along the river, for it was then the earth offered most of its bounty. Several species of salmon migrating upstream to their spawning grounds became the focus of activity in all the villages from spring through fall. Men speared the fish or dipped long-handled nets into the current while poised on rocks or pole scaffolds. Basket traps, seine nets, and weirs were used secondarily by the fishermen. Women butchered the fish, barbecuing some of the fresh fillets over an open fire or boiling it with roots. Most of the salmon was hung to dry in the wind and shade, then stacked in sheaves like wheat, to be stored for winter use or saved for trading. Some of the salmon was pulverized (sugared) to make an especially valued trade item.

The salmon harvest season was the time of heaviest trading, with the Wascos and Sahaptins performing the role of middlemen in a network that extended west to the coast, north into Canada, south into California, and east to the Rocky Mountains. Visitors from distant tribes camped with their hosts amid a festive atmosphere which also included catching up on news, sharing songs and dances, gambling, and courting. Trading was a friendly but formalized activity often carried out between regular trading partners. Dried salmon and other fish products were the river people's stock in trade, which they used to obtain: shells and roots from the west; baskets, beads, and blankets from the north; horses and buffalo hides from the east; and obsidian, bows and arrows, feathers, baskets and even slaves from the south. Trading was often complex, with goods changing hands many times.

For the Sahaptins in particular, there was much plant gathering to be done during the good months, and about half the population moved south for part or all of the season. Edible roots, ritually gathered in early spring, could still be dug through June, with other roots maturing later. Near the end of summer, huckleberries ripened in the mountains and chokecherries near the streams. The people pulled up cedar roots for bags, nets, and clothing, and picked black lichen from the boughs of pine and fir trees to pit-roast. Men hunted deer, elk, and smaller game, and women butchered them, leaving few parts unused: the meat was cooked fresh or smoked, the hides were tanned and used for clothing and bedding, the sinew for thread, the bones for needles, gorges, and fishhooks, and the antlers for

---

*The Wasco and Sahaptin languages, which belong to the Chinookan and Sahaptian language families, respectively, have been postulated to belong to a "Penutian" phylum that includes languages in eastern and western Oregon as well as California. Despite this classification and the geographic proximity of the two languages, Wasco and Sahaptin are mutually unintelligible.

114

various tools. Other animals—such as bear, wolf, coyote, cougar, otter, beaver, raccoon, and rabbit—provided skins and furs for household items or trade.

Hunting continued into the fall, with long expeditions up the tributaries. Fall was also the time to collect tule reeds and cattails from the riverbanks for use in constructing mat-covered shelters. Preparations for winter were made, including the collecting of firewood and the dismantling of the summer villages.

Life in the winter villages, which were set up in protected places away from the river, was more stationary but no less busy. Besides trapping, stream fishing, and collecting fuel, the Wascos and Sahaptins spent the winter making tools, weapons, clothing, and household items. Bone and plant fibers were the most commonly used materials, but the people also used wood to make canoes, digging sticks, arrow and spear shafts, fire drills, dipnet hoops, snowshoes, and cradleboards. The river people at the time of contact were not known to have engaged in metalworking or ceramics, and stone working was limited. Knives and projectile points fashioned from local basalt and obsidian have been found in great quantities along the Columbia, but it has been theorized that the later occupants borrowed the crafted items from the abandoned sites of earlier peoples or traded for them.* Some rocks were pecked into pestles, mauls, and hammers, but other rock tools like scrapers and net weights were used as they were found in nature.

Winter was a time for storytelling, as entertainment and instruction. Children huddled around the warm hearth, listening to tales of Coyote the Trickster, whose misbehavior served as a kind of negative role model, or Coyote the Changer, who was always present during critical transitions in the history of the river people. Through the telling of such tales, children learned about the geography and the flora and fauna of the physical world, while absorbing some of the values of their culture.

By late March, the winter villages made way for the summer fishing villages. The year's first roots and

salmon were collected ritually and blessed in a special spring ceremony and feast, for which the Sahaptins assembled at Tinainu. Huckleberries and venison were similarly celebrated in late summer. Such first-food ceremonies were carried out before the food could be eaten and the general harvest could begin, as a kind of atonement to the earth's spirits.

The spiritual lives of the Sahaptins and Wascos were inseparable from this daily routine. All beings, and inanimate objects as well, were assumed to have spirits or souls. The feasts were an acknowledgment of those spirits in nature and the people's cooperative and symmetrical relationship with them. A measure of the people's integration with the natural world was their practice of adopting animal spirits as their guardians, internalizing particular animals' powers and protection to help them through life. At the age of six or older, a boy or girl was sent out on a spirit quest, a nighttime encounter with the natural and supernatural worlds, which could result in the accepting of a guardian animal spirit and its song.

During the winter, people gathered for spirit dances, lasting several days at a time. At these ceremonies, people depicted their animal spirits in dance, to the sound of ritual singing and drumming. In this manner, others might become aware of the identity of a person's spirit, but not necessarily the nature of its powers.

Illness or death might result when a child's guardian spirit matured or became lost, or when one person's spirit entered another's body and battled with the host spirit. Then a shaman, who possessed many guardian spirits and therefore had much power at his disposal, might be called in to work on the victim. The shaman would draw out any intrusive or troublesome spirits, perhaps do battle with them himself, and either dispose of them or return them to the body where they belonged.

Shamans also played a role in administering justice in the Wasco and Sahaptin communities. Carefully screened and selected by other shamans before they were allowed to "practice," shamans were generally forthright, trustworthy men. They were therefore allowed to decide when a member of the community

---

* George Peter Murdock, "The Tenino Indians."

had gone too far, meting out punishment (illness or death) with their sorcery. Occasionally bad shamans abused their power by carrying out personal acts of revenge, often on other shamans, but the community was vigilant and intolerant of such abuse.

At death, people's spirits left their bodies and traveled to a spirit world in the west; disembodied spirits might come back to retrace their steps or otherwise haunt their former world. Archaeological evidence shows a certain attention to detail in burials, perhaps to ensure that the spirit of the deceased would rest quietly and be prepared for the next world. The body was wrapped in buckskin and, along with some valuables, was taken to a burial site away from the village, often on an island in the Columbia. Wascos placed their dead in communal burial houses above the ground, while Sahaptins were more apt to bury underground, sometimes within a wood frame chamber. Some elders on the reservation today report that the body was unearthed and the bones rewrapped after about a year. The mourning rituals are a little less certain, but it is believed that burial was preceded by two or three days of singing and dancing to give the body a chance to come back to life, although this practice may have developed rather late in the pre-contact period. In the days after the burial, Wascos and perhaps Sahaptins performed such rituals as cutting survivors' hair short and taking purifying sweat baths.

The extended family was the basic economic and social unit. Marriages usually occurred between men and women of comparable social standing, and weddings involved long and ritualized gift exchanges between families. Men often took more than one wife, but there were taboos against adultery and incest. The primary care of children was the woman's responsibility, with grandmothers also assuming active roles. Often an individual outside the family would be invited to help in the preparation of children for adulthood, and at social or religious gatherings, children might be disciplined by a community "whipman." This communal aspect to child-rearing instilled in children the notion of respecting and listening carefully to all their elders, who had much to teach them about survival and ethics.

Two families, whose male heads were often related, usually shared a hearth and some food supplies, with as many as thirty people occupying a single dwelling. Their earthen-floored homes were round or oblong pole structures covered with tule mats. The Wascos often used wood planks for siding and built their structures partly underground, as their coastal relatives did. Between seven and twenty households usually comprised a village.

Each village had its headman, who was either descended from a headman or possessed special skills. Among the Wascos, wealth was also a factor, as measured by the amount of salmon stored away, or the number of wives or slaves. The headman was assisted by lesser headmen, but there was no formal hierarchy or political organization. Headmen, or chiefs as they were later called by white men, were not decision-makers as much as they were moral guides and advisers to the community. Decisions were usually made by group consensus, with the aid of this advice.

Villages were fairly independent. Although there was acknowledgement of the common bond of culture, language, and economy, there was no real political federation of either the Sahaptin or Wasco villages.

SURVIVING IN THE GREAT BASIN

At the southernmost limit of the river people's seasonal travels, they encountered another people who roamed in search of many of the same foods. These inhabitants of the dry interior of what is now Oregon spoke yet another tongue and had a cultural tradition quite distinct from their northern neighbors. Without the salmon of the river people, and removed from the center of trade on the Columbia, the Northern Paiutes had to roam widely to satisfy their needs for food, clothing, and shelter. Theirs was a tough and portable culture, with little organization beyond the family group.

The Paiutes were a Shoshonean people who spoke an Uto-Aztecan language linking them distantly with the Hopi of the Southwest and the ancient Aztecs of Mexico. Their heartland was that portion of the vast Great Basin that lay in southeastern Oregon and

A *turn-of-the-century tule mat lodge along the Columbia River shows the evolution from a traditional, rounded shape to a peaked, Plains-style design. Clothing, too, had changed by this time to reflect the style of the surrounding white culture. (OHS neg. 44160)*

northwestern Nevada. It was a semi-arid region that seemed utterly inhospitable to the white people who hurried past to the north and south on their way to western Oregon's farmland and California's gold in the first half of the nineteenth century. But the Paiutes had developed a fragile adaptation to their difficult land, and they defended it whenever it was threatened.

The Northern Paiutes shared a rather vague and shifting territorial boundary with the Sahaptin and Wasco peoples at about the same latitude as the present Warm Springs Reservation, and skirmishes between hunting and gathering parties from the north and south were not uncommon. There was some trading between the two peoples, but such valued goods as slaves and horses were more likely to be taken by

force. It is unknown how long antagonism existed between the river and basin peoples, but with the expansion southward of the Sahaptins and the later pressure of white settlement on both groups, conflict must have at least intensified in the nineteenth century.

Simply having enough to eat was cause for celebration for the Northern Paiutes, who named themselves after the foods on which they most depended. In Oregon, there were such groups as the *Wadadika* (seed-eaters) of the Harney Valley-Malheur Lake area, the *Hunibuidika* (root-eaters) to the north on the John Day River, and the *Wadihichidika* (juniper- and deer-eaters) along the Deschutes and Crooked rivers in central Oregon. It was the Wadihichidika whom the river tribes probably encountered most frequently and it

117

The Northern Paiutes depended on the seeds of the water lily (wokas), which they collected using small tule reed boats, or less frequently, with dug-outs like these Klamath canoes. (The Smithsonian Institution neg. no. 3061-E-2)

was in a corner of their territory that the Warm Springs Reservation was established. Descendants of several Northern Paiute groups live on the reservation today.

The people of the Great Basin, despite their regional specialties and their marked decentralization, shared a common culture with a material and spiritual orientation shaped by a harsh environment. The Great Basin, once a land of many lakes, has for centuries been a high desert of sparse vegetation and extreme temperatures. Its native residents were a hardy, practical people.

Each spring, the year-round dryness of central and southeastern Oregon was spelled by the run-off from melting snow in the mountains. Streams rose and the ancient lakebeds filled, creating vast wetlands that teemed with life. Cattail shoots were one of the first edible signs of spring. The people ventured into the marshes in small tule reed or wooden dugout boats, collecting plants and luring ducks and other waterfowl with tule decoys. Men took to the streams and caught suckers, trout, and some salmon with willow traps or trays, and to a lesser extent with spears. Some of the catch was eaten fresh, but much was dried and put away. Spring was also the time for women to dig up the edible roots of several desert plants, which were eaten fresh or dried and cached for later use.

The busy schedule of gathering and preserving the spring bounty brought families together in communal work groups. But as the heat of summer approached, the families went their separate ways in pursuit of several kinds of berries and seeds, scarce water, small game, and insects such as crickets, grasshoppers, and ants. The Paiutes were often referred to pejoratively as "Digger" Indians by white people who witnessed but did not appreciate their dependence on whatever nature had to offer.

Autumn was another rich time for the Paiutes, providing (depending on the locale) the seeds of the water lily and sunflower, pine nuts, rabbits, deer, and antelope. This tended to be the biggest communal gathering of the year, a social time of dancing, gaming, and courting as well as a time for hard work. Rabbit drives were organized, with both men and women flushing jackrabbits or cottontails into long sagebrush-twine nets. Deer and antelope were brought in by the men, and the women cooked or dried the meat and tanned the hides. Pine nuts and seeds were gathered, roasted, and ground for later use in gruel.

By November, it was time to gather up cached food and select sites for winter camps near water and away from the elements. A few families might winter together, sharing food with each other and with nearby camps that might run short. The cold months were a time for wrapping in rabbitskin blankets, staying close to the fire, telling stories, and making tools and household items.

With willow gathered from streamsides, the women twined conical burden baskets, winnowing trays, seed beaters, water jugs, bowls and utensils, and cradleboards. From the inner bark of sagebrush, they fashioned skirts, shirts, leggings, and capes, but these items of clothing were also sewn from buckskin if it was available. Men sewed their own buckskin quivers, and constructed their arrows from hard berry wood and obsidian points and their bows from juniper and sinew. Stone implements like axes, clubs, and pestles were pecked from available stone.

In their constant search for food, water, and fuel, the Paiutes constructed only temporary homes. Their winter shelters were usually domed willow frames covered with mats of tule, cattail or sagebrush, and resting on top of the ground. In the warmer, more transient months, shelter was as basic as a mat-covered lean-to or simply a brush enclosure to deflect the wind.

Equally simple was the Paiutes' political and social organization. Because they had to cover so much ground to collect the food and raw materials they needed, the extended family was the most efficient grouping through most of the year. When it came time for the people to gather in larger work groups, leaders might be selected for a specific event or task, such as the rabbit drive. Otherwise, there was little need for leadership beyond the sage advice of an elder or someone with a special skill or insight.

Ritual was spare, too, among the Paiutes. Fathers held short, quiet ceremonies for their sons when they killed their first deer, and girls followed prescribed procedures when they first menstruated, including isolation. Courtship was rather perfunctory, and marriage itself even more so. A brief flirtation might culminate in the boy making nightly visits to the girl's home until she agreed to lie with him. There was no formal wedding and gift exchange. The ideal husband was a good hunter and provider and the ideal wife was a good cook and a gentle personality. Men frequently had more than one wife. At death, a person's body was washed and dressed in his best clothes, then taken far from the camp and placed under a pile of rocks.

The natural world of the Paiute was as alive with spirits as that of the river people, but the powers associated with animals seemed to be the province of the shamans and not of each individual. Shamans were active dreamers who uncovered problems and found cures while in the dream state. Using such paraphernalia as eagle feathers and deer-hoof rattles, they cured physical or emotional ailments with singing, dancing and physical extraction of the offending spirit. They also controlled the weather and could be hired to "poison" a person.

The spiritual lives of the Northern Paiutes may not have seemed fertile enough to give rise to the prophecy and ritual of the Ghost Dance, which swept the Great Basin in the late nineteenth century. Nor did their practical adaptation to the high desert landscape

119

suggest the need for any physical or spiritual change. But the introduction of a new element—white settlement—threw their carefully balanced lives off center and proved how vulnerable a hardy people can be.

THE NEWCOMERS

Both the Columbia River and the Great Basin people predicted the coming of a different kind of human being. According to the prophecies, it was to be an event ranging from benign to blessed. At least one group of Northern Paiutes told of a noisy people with a different language coming from the east and bringing with them an animal (the horse) and chokecherries as big as a fist (the apple).* In the northern Plateau area, a prophet of the Spokan tribe uttered this poignant prediction in the late eighteenth century:

> Soon there will come from the rising sun a different kind of man from any you have yet seen, who will bring with them a book and will teach you everything, and after that the world will fall to pieces.†

This prophecy may not have had the ominous intent it now imparts, because the end of the world was expected to bring perpetual bliss to the river people. But, as it turned out, the prophecy was fulfilled quite literally—their world did fall to pieces—and the millennium has yet to begin.

Years before actual contact with the newcomers, the natives of the river and basin felt their presence. The early 1700s were marked by the arrival from the south of the horse, which had been introduced to the New World by Spaniards about two hundred years before. Sometime during the eighteenth century Euro-American trade goods, such as beads, blankets, and metalware began to appear from the coastal region. And by the end of of that century, a smattering of Christian (specifically Catholic) rituals had made their

---

*Beatrice Blyth Whiting, *Paiute Sorcery*.
†Christopher Miller, *Prophetic Worlds*.

way west through the trade network.

The middle Columbia, busy as it was in Indian trade circles, was somewhat isolated from the early activities of non-Indians in the Northwest, and the Great Basin was of little interest to whites until more than halfway through the nineteenth century. West of the Cascade Mountains, however, the natives of the coast and lower Columbia had had contact with European and American beaver trappers for at least a dozen years before Lewis and Clark came down the river. These fur traders reported signs of smallpox, a Euro-American disease, among the native population, evidence of earlier contact with coastal explorers. Fur traders seem to have crossed the Rocky Mountains into the eastern Plateau region about the same time. But it was not until 1805, with the arrival of Lewis and Clark that the mid-Columbia people had their first face-to-face contact with whites.

The people of the river, accustomed to having visits from other native groups, looked upon the new people as just another kind of visitor with new and different trade items. The explorers and Indians both grumbled about thievery, high prices, or poor quality merchandise, but they continued to do business and to satisfy some portion of their cultural curiosity about one another. While Lewis and Clark commented on the "dirty" conditions they found among the natives, they did not hesitate to socialize or share food with them. Members of the expedition were often invited, or invited themselves, into the river people's lodges, where they presented small gifts and shared smokes with their hosts. The natives, in turn, enjoyed visiting the white men's camp, where they found amusement in the fiddling and dancing of the strange new culture.

Contact between whites and natives was sporadic until missionaries arrived in The Dalles in 1838. With the establishment of Methodist missions at The Dalles and upriver at Walla Walla, the non-Indian presence was changing. The transience of traders and explorers was giving way to the permanence of white settlers. The river and plateau country became a byway for the ever-increasing flow of settlers to western Oregon,

1,000 in 1843 and 11,000–12,000 in 1852.* Eventually, the mid-Columbia was a stopping point itself for people who wanted more than salmon, dog meat, or berries. They wanted the land for farming, and as they settled on the Indians' hunting and gathering grounds, they put pressure on the prior occupants to either be gone or, if they must live nearby, to be more civilized.

When Christian women and children joined their menfolk, it became a matter of great importance to change the natives' dress, hygiene, cultural behavior, and economic patterns, as well as their spiritual beliefs. The trappings of western civilization were earthly manifestations of the Christian God, and it was no use teaching the Scriptures without modifying the natives' life-style. Some Indians, particularly the Wascos, took up farming on a small scale, adopted the trousers and calico dresses of the settlers, and began developing a rudimentary understanding of English.

The first missionaries at The Dalles found a number of Christian elements in the natives' rituals, such as observance of the Sabbath, kneeling, and saying grace at mealtime. Seen by the missionaries as evidence of God's universal work, it increased their fervor and their expectations. The natives, too, had expectations. These Bible-carrying white men could be the ones to "teach (them) everything," as in the prophecy. But with the "book" they also brought settlers, soldiers, and disruption. The river people were soon disenchanted.

The newcomers' zealous efforts to uplift the "heathens" were also undermined by the introduction of deadly alcohol and disease. The Indian people had no immunity to either, and each took its toll. Smallpox swept through the tribes, not with the same devastation as the tribes of western Oregon experienced, but with demoralizing effects. Alcohol was a slower killer, seeping into the culture and claiming its victims even today.

Two years after the Oregon Territory was established in 1848, the Oregon Land Donation Act promised 320 acres in the territory to any adult U. S. citizen, resulting in another influx and further conflicts over land. Some Warm Springs people today feel that hostilities were exaggerated or even invented in order to justify the removal of Indians from the river and prime farming land, but the massacre at the Whitman mission in Walla Walla in 1847 and the murder of several Indians near Fort Dalles in 1854 were indicators of growing tension.

A particularly well-educated Wasco named William ("Billy") Chinook, who had traveled and lived in the East, escorted by explorer John Fremont, expressed his people's frustration in an 1853 letter to a government official. He wrote:

> We are tormented almost every day by the white people who desire to settle on our land and although we have built houses and opened gardens they wish in spite of us to take possession of the very spots we occupy. . . . Now we wish to know whether this is the land of the white mans or the Indians. If it is our land the white must not trouble us. If it is the land of the white man when did he buy it? †

The next year, Joel Palmer, superintendent of Indian Affairs for the Oregon Territory, interpreted the problem in a letter to the commissioner of Indian Affairs in Washington, D. C. "Much of the present difficulty," he wrote, "is traceable to the mistaken policy of permitting the settlement of this country prior to the extinguishment of the Indian title and the designation of proper reservations."††

There is no indication in either the Palmer or the Chinook letter of the fundamentally different way in which the two cultures originally perceived the land in question. Palmer apparently assumed, perhaps for the government's convenience in acquiring it, that Indians held title to their land. While the natives had fairly well-defined territories that they inhabited, the notion

---

* David French, *Wasco-Wishram*.

† A copy of this letter is in the possession of the Confederated Tribes.

†† Palmer's letter appears in Thelma Drake Cliff's "A History of Warm Springs Reservation, 1855–1900.

of land ownership was traditionally unfamiliar to them. These contrasting assumptions created much misunderstanding during the settlement period, but Chinook's letter shows that by 1853, at least some of the river people understood the concept of land purchase. What Palmer and Chinook were both objecting to was the common view that the land in the Oregon Territory was free for the taking, that any rights the native inhabitants had to it were of little or no consequence.

The gathering momentum of westward expansion meant an inevitable increase in settlers' claims to the river people's lands. In Palmer's mind, it would be a more orderly process if the government would frame treaties of land cession and convince the Indians that it was in their interest to sign.

The resultant "Treaty with the Tribes of Middle Oregon, 1855" was one of a series of nearly identical treaties made by the U. S. Government with other river tribes during June of that year. But it was also part of a much larger national trend to remove Indian tribes from favorable land and place them on reservations. Before the treaty-making period ended in 1871, 370 treaties had ceded countless acres of aboriginal land throughout the United States and its territories, reserving 138 million acres (or about six percent of the present U.S. land base) for the use of Indian tribes.

In the Oregon Territory, with its own superintendent of Indian affairs and treaty-making commission, the purchase of native lands had started in earnest around 1851. The tribes of western Oregon were first on the agenda, since the lush, fertile land they occupied was most desirable to the settlers. These tribes and the tribes of eastern Oregon successfully resisted the superintendent's original plan, which was to move the western Oregon Indians to the east side of the Cascades; but they watched helplessly as whole sections of the coast and the inland valleys were lost with a few strokes of the pen. Several early treaties were never ratified by Congress, and the temporary reservations assigned to the tribes were later whittled away.

The summer of 1855 was a busy time for Superintendent Palmer, who had been left with much unfinished business by the previous superintendent. In June alone, he oversaw two major treaty councils that resulted in four treaties with the mid-Columbia tribes. At the Walla Walla Council, Palmer signed treaties with the Cayuse, who went to the Umatilla Reservation, and with the Nez Perce, who had land reserved in both Oregon and Idaho. At the Wasco Council, he treated with the "tribes of middle Oregon," creating the Warm Springs Reservation. (Washington Territorial Governor Isaac Stevens also signed a treaty that month with the Wishram and Sahaptin people on the north side of the Columbia, establishing the Yakima Reservation.) By September Palmer had persuaded all the coastal tribes to sign away their lands; the tribes of the upper Willamette Valley had ceded their land the previous January. Considerably weakened and depleted by smallpox, tuberculosis, and other introduced diseases, as well as by the starvation that resulted when their foraging lands were fenced off and zealously defended, most of the tribes of the Oregon Territory resisted the treaties only with poignant oratory. The land cessions were a foregone conclusion and the Indians seemed to know it.

But it was with troubled hearts that representatives of three bands of Wascos—the Dog River (Hood River), Dalles, and Ki-gal-twal-la—and four bands of "Walla Wallas"—the Upper Deschutes (Tygh), Lower Deschutes (Wyam), Tenino, and John Day—signed the Treaty with the Tribes of Middle Oregon. Some families among both the Wascos and Sahaptins refused to sign and went on living along the Columbia, unprotected by federal law.

The Treaty of 1855 ceded ten million acres of land that roughly corresponded to the territory used by the river tribes—from the Cascade Mountains on the west to Willow Creek and the Blue Mountains on the east, and from the channel of the Columbia south to the 44th parallel. Within that ceded area, about one hundred miles south of the Columbia, 578,000 acres were reserved for the exclusive use of the river people. Unwanted by white settlers and only occasionally visited by the river tribes, the reserved land lay in an area frequented by the Northern Paiutes.

In return for the cession, the tribes were to receive one hundred fifty thousand dollars (or about two cents an acre) not in cash but in tools, clothing, provisions,

122

The 1855 Treaty with the Tribes of Middle Oregon was a hastily written document, but its longhand prose has held up in courts throughout the last century. (National Archives)

and salaried employees for the reservation. The government further promised to construct a variety of buildings, including a sawmill, flouring mill, blacksmith shop, gunsmith shop, and a wagon and plowmaker shop, as well as homes for each of the personnel running these operations. For each of the four chiefs designated in the treaty, the government also planned to build a home on ten plowed and fenced acres of land, and to pay an annual salary of five hundred dollars to the head chief for twenty years—no doubt a selling point of the treaty.

Perhaps the most valued aspect of the treaty was the reserving of the people's right to fish at "usual and accustomed stations" and to hunt and gather "on unclaimed lands." This meant there could be at least some continuity in the people's lives, although access to these sites became more and more difficult in the decades to follow.

What the government asked for in return, in addition to the land, was the peacefulness and cooperation of the tribes. They were to acknowledge their dependence on the government, observe all U.S. laws, rules, and regulations prescribed for them, be friendly with U. S. citizens, and refrain from going to war with other tribes. Between the lines of the treaty was the expectation that the Indians would benefit from the government's introduction of civilization to the reservation. With payments and services due to end twenty years after settlement of the reservation, there was a clear assumption: that the Indians would be ready and willing to fend for themselves on completely new terms long before the end of the century.

Treaty-making in the Northwest was not entirely successful. The Sahaptin leader Kamiakin regretted almost immediately having signed the Yakima Treaty, and began to gather followers (including a number from Warm Springs) and to whip up resentment that erupted in the Yakima War of 1855—56. The Nez Perces' Oregon reservation was lost to an Idaho treaty in 1863, launching the celebrated resistance and flight into Canada led by Chief Joseph. Nor was treaty-making finished in Oregon by 1855. There was still the vast interior of the territory to "tame."

For the most part, the undesirability of the southeastern portion of Oregon kept the pressure off the natives until the 1860s. In 1864, the Klamaths and Modocs signed a treaty bringing the antagonistic tribes together on the Klamath Reservation in south-central Oregon. A few Northern Paiutes signed, but most were still at large in their huge homeland, beginning to feel the effects of the white presence. The establishment of the Warm Springs Reservation on their northwestern boundary and the settlement of white ranchers and miners in the late 1860s on some of their most valuable food gathering areas—around Harney Lake and on the Deschutes and John Day rivers—put the Paiutes on the defensive. The equilibrium of their marginal existence on the dry, harsh land was easily upset and their response was to roam more widely and raid frequently.

One of the most active of the raiding Paiute bands was led by the notorious Paulina (*Panaina*), whose attacks on both the Warm Springs Reservation and white settlements in central Oregon are legendary. Though he signed an 1865 treaty adding more land to the Klamath Reservation, he stayed there for less than a year. In 1867, the U.S. Army, led by Lt. William C. McKay and assisted by seventy Warm Springs scouts, set out after him in earnest, but it was a fatal encounter with a rancher three months later that ended Paulina's career.

The following year, the Northern Paiutes remaining in Oregon signed a peace treaty but it was not until 1872 that an executive order from the President established the 1.7 million acre Malheur Indian Reservation near the present town of Burns. Ten years later, the reservation was returned to the public domain because it was uninhabited. Many Paiutes had gone to live on other reservations in Oregon and Nevada while waiting for their own reservation. Then in 1878, a number of Paiutes joined the Bannocks from Idaho in retaliating against the U. S. Army, but they were soon captured and held at Fort Vancouver in Washington or ordered to live on the Yakima Reservation. In 1879, an agreement was reached with Warm Springs for thirty-eight Paiutes to settle on the south end of their reser-

Mt. Jefferson stands at the southwestern corner of the Warm Springs Reservation, rising above a land of sagebrush, timber, rivers, and canyons. Locals say its double peak represents a canoe stranded during the big flood. (Cynthia D. Stowell)

vation, in an area called Seekseequa. They were later joined by more than seventy Paiutes from Yakima.

It was an uneasy marriage at first, this sharing of the reservation by longtime enemies. Though they were not treaty-signers, the Paiutes were extended all the rights and privileges of the Warm Springs and Wascos, and today they are one of the three tribes making up the Confederated Tribes of the Warm Springs Reservation of Oregon.

THE NEW LAND

It was a trek like so many others in the nineteenth century, since the federal government had begun removing Indian tribes from the path of pioneering Americans. The Wishrams and Sahaptins on the north side of the Columbia, like many tribes across the continent, had to be forced by the U.S. Army onto the Yakima Reservation; but those on the south side moved peacefully to the Warm Springs Reservation, a com-

paratively short journey, to land that was on the fringes of the river people's traditional territory. In fact, the trail they walked to the new reservation was a well-established route along the Deschutes River that connected their hunting and gathering grounds to the Columbia. But despite the relative ease of the move, the people's footsteps must have been heavy as they turned their backs on their homeland and way of life.

There is some disagreement among contemporary residents of the reservation about who arrived first, but other than a few Sahaptins at large with Kamiakin and his resistance, the move was virtually complete before the treaty was ratified by Congress in 1859. The Wascos settled in and near the valley which is now the town of Warm Springs; then, as now, it was the site of the Bureau of Indian Affairs (BIA) Agency. The Tenino band of Sahaptins settled near the Agency along what came to be known as Tenino Creek. Other Sahaptin bands established settlements on the north end of the reservation, around the present hamlet of Simnasho.

The land was hard to dislike. The reservation was, and is, a land of gentle, sage-covered hills, dramatic rock formations, steep canyons, hot mineral springs, pine and fir forests, mountain peaks, and clean, rushing water. The eastern half is a land given over to the brown tones of hot, dry summers and cold winters, but with a brief soft greening in spring and a yellow profusion of sage blossoms in the autumn. The timbered foothills and mountains to the west and north offer cool, green relief and watersheds for streams.

The newcomers to the reservation found the game, roots, and berries that had helped sustain them for millennia, although for many years they preferred to return to their more familiar haunts to gather food. Trout, steelhead, and salmon filled the reservation's rivers and streams, but nothing could match the flavor and volume of the Columbia River catch, which the people continued to pursue in the traditional manner until Celilo Falls was inundated in 1957. Zealous government workers tried during the early years of the reservation to make farmers of the Indians, but most of the land, except along the rivers and streams, was not well-suited to agriculture. It would be nearly a cen-

tury before the Confederated Tribes would begin to actively exploit the reservation's natural resources.

The whole relationship of the river tribes to the land was altered when the reservation was established. Not only did they have to transfer their allegiance to a parcel of land that figured little into their culture, history, and accustomed lifestyle, they also had to learn new ways of inhabiting and using their land. Indians throughout North America made little distinction between themselves and the natural world; humans, animals, plants, and the soil itself had spirits that interacted as part of a harmonious whole. The land could be used, with proper displays of respect and gratefulness, but it never occurred to the native people that it could be owned.

The treaty of 1855 and subsequent laws and court decisions changed all that. It was an erroneous but convenient assumption on the part of the United States that the Indians held "title" to the territory they inhabited. Once this relationship was described in European, legalistic terms, it could be extinguished.

The Warm Springs Reservation, like other Indian reservations, was not *granted* by the government; rather, it was *retained* by the treaty tribes as part of their aboriginal territory. But it was on different terms. The government legally held title to the new reservation in much the same way a minor's bank account is held in trust by a parent. To this day, it is the government's responsibility to manage the reservation land for the benefit of the treaty tribes. This "trust responsibility" has been interpreted more broadly through the years to include federal responsibility for the general welfare of Indian tribes, but the protection of their land base and resources continues to be at the heart of the special relationship that exists between Indians and the United States.

Trusteeship may also have been intended as a kind of gentle introduction of the river tribes to land ownership, but it no doubt hindered the development of any proprietary feelings toward the new land. Neither has the government's trust responsibility always guaranteed protection of the land base. Many reservations have lost huge portions of their acreage or have been

126

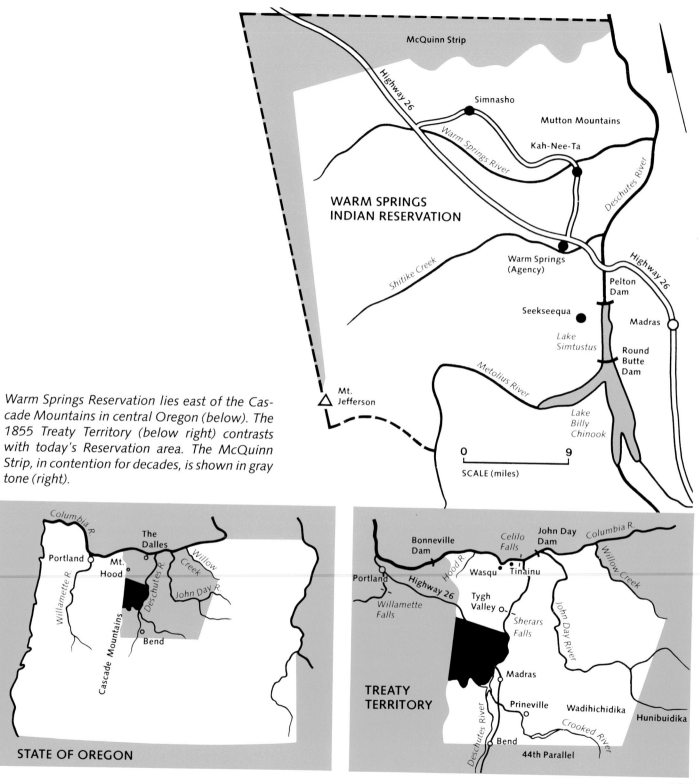

Warm Springs Reservation lies east of the Cascade Mountains in central Oregon (below). The 1855 Treaty Territory (below right) contrasts with today's Reservation area. The McQuinn Strip, in contention for decades, is shown in gray tone (right).

McQuinn Strip

Highway 26

Simnasho

Mutton Mountains

Kah-Nee-Ta

Warm Springs River

Deschutes River

WARM SPRINGS
INDIAN RESERVATION

Shitike Creek

Warm Springs
(Agency)

Highway 26

Pelton
Dam

Seekseequa

Madras

Lake
Simtustus

Round
Butte
Dam

Metolius River

Mt.
Jefferson

Lake
Billy
Chinook

0   9

SCALE (miles)

STATE OF OREGON

Columbia R.

The Dalles

Portland

Mt.
Hood

Willow Creek

Deschutes R.

John Day R.

Willamette R.

Cascade Mountains

Bend

TREATY
TERRITORY

Columbia R.

Bonneville
Dam

Celilo
Falls

John Day
Dam

Willow Creek

Portland

Highway 26

Hood R.

Wasqu

Tinainu

Willamette
Falls

Tygh
Valley

Sherars
Falls

John Day River

Madras

Prineville

Wadihichidika

Hunibuidika

Deschutes River

Crooked River

Bend

44th Parallel

127

terminated altogether as Congress and courts have responded to pressures from white citizens. Warm Springs has been fortunate throughout the assaults, and its acreage has remained intact. Actually, with annexations and the settlement of a long-term boundary dispute, the Warm Springs Reservation is now larger than it was when the Sahaptins and Wascos began settling it more than a century ago.

While initially resenting confinement on the somewhat unfamiliar land, the people of the river have come to identify strongly with the geographical borders that define their lives. Forming the eastern boundary of the 640,000-acre reservation is the Deschutes River, which flows north into the Columbia. The southern boundary is formed in part by the Metolius River, which flows east into the Deschutes. Snowcapped Mt. Jefferson, its peak a legendary canoe stranded after the Great Flood, stands at the southwestern corner. The western boundary line follows the crest of the Cascade Mountains and meets the northern boundary at a much disputed point that went unresolved until 1972. Along the northern boundary are the rugged and forbidding Mutton Mountains, which some locals believe are inhabited by a huge, hairy humanoid known throughout the Northwest as "Bigfoot." The Warm Springs River traverses the interior, originating in the mountains and spilling into the Deschutes, carving canyons and valleys along the way and providing spawning grounds for salmon, steelhead, and trout. State Highway 26 also bisects the reservation, connecting central Oregon with Portland and the Willamette Valley, and putting the Warm Springs people in more direct contact with the "outside" world than was ever expected when the reservation was set aside.

When compared with other Indian reservations, the Warm Springs Reservation is average to small in size. But what it lacks in acreage, it makes up for in resources. The land set aside for the river tribes as unfavorable for settlement by white people has since proved to be the Tribes' biggest asset, along with the intelligent leadership that has guided its development.

Timber covers more than half the reservation, with ponderosa pine at the lower elevations and Douglas fir and other species in the higher and wetter elevations.

Managed by the BIA, and commercially exploited by a tribal enterprise, this resource now provides the Tribes with their principal industry and income. The rivers of the reservation have also proven profitable, with rental monies accruing from two utility-owned dams and income being realized from a new tribal hydroelectric project. And the beauty of the land has made tourism a natural enterprise for the Tribes.

The people of the Warm Springs Reservation are clearly bound to their land in a new and different way. Sometimes that bond is expressed in a fierce pride and protectiveness, other times in cool-headed planning. The reservation may not be their original home, but it feels like home to the descendants of the Columbia River and Great Basin peoples. It is the place on earth where they feel the most comfortable. No matter how their relationship with the land has changed, the people understand that their survival as an economic, political, and even cultural group depends on this reservation land base and its wise use.

THE PEOPLE TODAY

Descendants of the displaced people who settled into their new reservation life more than a century ago live on the same land today with a stronger community identity than ever. Calling themselves the "Confederated Tribes of the Warm Springs Reservation of Oregon," they are a corporation and a government, as well as a people with a shared geography, history, and culture. From an estimated 1,000–1,400 fishermen, hunters, and gatherers, the reservation population has grown to 2,800 individuals engaged in all manner of pursuits: they are accountants, administrators, entrepreneurs, millworkers, truck drivers, secretaries, counselors, lifeguards . . . there is even an ombudsman.

Life is not as simple as it was when family, village, the natural world, and the spirit world were the sole parameters. Now, reservation life has been complicated by twenty million dollar tribal budgets, federal regulations, attorney fees, and management plans. It is a life that in many ways mirrors the white culture that has come to surround and overshadow the native cul-

128

ture. But, as much as the Tribes engage the world outside the reservation, the people still live apart, isolated by physical and psychological boundaries that accentuate their original differentness.

On the Warm Springs Reservation, people of three separate cultures have learned to think of themselves as one; as tribal differences narrowed, political and economic strength became a priority. Granted, the Sahaptin bands, who came to be known as the Warm Springs tribe, still identify with the Simnasho area, the Wascos still think of Agency as their stronghold, and many Paiutes still live at Seekseequa. In fact, these "districts" were institutionalized in the composition of the Tribal Council when the Tribal Constitution was framed in the 1930s. But that constitution also created a business entity and a government that brought the three tribes together.

Reservation history has been short. One needs only to recognize today's surnames among the names listed on the treaty or see contemporary family resemblances in the faces preserved on nineteenth-century glass negatives to understand the brevity. It is understandable, then, that families have had difficulty forgetting early tribal antagonisms. How can a Wasco forget that her great-grandmother was captured by renegade Paiutes, or how can a Warm Springs or Paiute individual forget that his family was shunned by Wascos for being "backward?" The people of Warm Springs have tried to put aside these memories and differences when the good of the Confederated Tribes as a whole is at stake, which is frequently.

Since the phenomenon of a single tribal entity is fairly new, formal membership has also been a recent development. Censuses were taken regularly after the reservation was settled. The first attempts to formulate a membership roll came in the 1880s when reservation personnel tried to implement a federal policy of allotting land to individuals to encourage farming. The allotment list of 1902, skewed by mixed blood and the presence of visiting relatives from other reservations, served for decades as a base roll. A new base membership roll completed by the tribal vital statistics department in 1979 centered on the 1940 census, but the 1902 list was still used as a research tool.

The Tribal Constitution of 1938, along with subsequent amendments, now provides for an orderly system of adding new members. Children of one-fourth or more "blood" of the Confederated Tribes who are born to members maintaining residence on the reservation at the time of birth are "automatic" members. Even the parents of automatic members, however, must file an application which undergoes the scrutiny of the vital statistics department. An individual with a lower blood quantum can become a member through the adoption process, a more subjective determination made by tribal voters in a referendum every few years. Applicants for adoption must have at least one-eighth Indian blood (any tribe), be descended from a member, have resided on the reservation at least three years, and not be a member of any other Indian tribe. Once they are cleared by the vital statistics office, their names go onto a ballot for an election that has been described variously as a popularity contest and an arena for family disputes. When persons become members, they can be disenrolled only at their own request, although there have been a handful of cases where processing mistakes were made and membership was revoked.

According to the vital statistics department, in 1985 there were 2,735 members of the Confederated Tribes, about 2,100 of whom lived on the reservation. It is a very young population, with almost half under the age of twenty and only three percent in the over-sixty bracket. Although the population declined for a time in the late nineteenth century, it has grown steadily in this century, with accelerated growth in the last few decades. About one hundred new members are enrolled each year, all but a handful by birth. This means that babies are being born at Warm Springs at about twice the national rate. Growth in tribal membership is tempered by about twenty-five deaths per year, on a par with the national death rate. But the average age at death, which was 37.6 years during the period 1979–1983,* is significantly lower than in the general population.

---

* Confederated Tribes, "Community Alcohol and Drug Task Force Proposal"

129

The colorful flag of the Confederated Tribes of Warm Springs, designed by tribal member Hamilton Greeley, flies alongside the American flag as an expression of the unity of the Wasco, Warm Springs, and Paiute people and the strength of their tribal government. (Confederated Tribes of Warm Springs)

Like members of other federally recognized tribes, members of the Confederated Tribes of Warm Springs are citizens of two nations—their tribal group and the United States. Both citizenships mean a great deal to them, as symbolized by the side-by-side display of American and tribal flags on buildings and at ceremonial occasions. Even before Indians became U.S. citizens in 1924, Warm Springs men volunteered in great numbers for military service during wartime. But the more immediate of the two allegiances is to the Confederated Tribes. Tribal membership not only means a share in tribal profits, participation in reservation politics and planning, and the right to inherit land on the reservation; it also means recognition as an Indian by the federal government, and therefore, entitlement to a whole realm of health, social service, and educational benefits. Less tangibly, membership provides an individual with a source of identity, pride, and social acceptance. Members may be eyed more seriously as mates and potential parents, their opinions on reservation issues are more valuable, and their prospects for employment on the reservation are greater.

As a citizen of the United States, a Warm Springs Indian has the same rights and responsibilities as any other citizen, including protection by the U.S. Constitution and its Bill of Rights, the right to vote, and the mandatory payment of personal federal income tax. The myth of the non-taxpaying Indian probably derives from two facts: reservation Indians generally do not pay state income taxes, and tribal business income and property are not taxable. Both of these exemptions are commonly viewed as part of the bargain struck with the federal government when aboriginal lands were relinquished. They are also recognition of the tribes' special relationship with the federal government as well as their existence as sovereign powers prior to the formation of states.

While it is true that Indian citizens benefit personally from certain rights reserved for them in their tribes' treaties, and from subsequent interpretations of the government's "trust responsibility" for Indian tribes and lands, these rights and privileges are tribal, not individual, rights. It is by virtue of their membership in a federally recognized tribe, and not due to any "super-citizenship," that Warm Springs Indians have access to free medical care, educational opportunities, protected off-reservation hunting and fishing, and other privileges and services not available to (and often begrudged by) non-Indian citizens.

Warm Springs Indians have more advantages than many other Indians because of the Tribes' successful business ventures. Many outsiders assume that the relative prosperity comes from government generosity, when, in fact, monthly per capita payments and year-end "bonuses" are made from tribal income, and such amenities as new housing, public works projects, and social service programs are provided by tribal funds, supplemented at times by federal subsidies available to any local government.

"The Indians have got it easy" is a sentiment frequently voiced by non-Indians who are bitter about opportunities available to the Warm Springs people. It is a mistake to think that they have not paid a price for this special status. They have paid with their land, their autonomy, and their culture. They have paid with the lives lost in the rush to twentieth century American culture, and with pride sacrificed to an overprotective trustee. The people of Warm Springs, who more than most other tribes control their own destiny, continue to suffer the consequences of having their way of life so severely disrupted more than a hundred years ago. □

131

BEFORE BOOMTOWN AND BEYOND

NATIVE PEOPLES UPROOTED from their land lose far more than the comfort of familiar surroundings. Displaced from a natural environment that has shaped and defined them for generations, they are apt to lose the whole focus of their economy, and ultimately, of their culture. This was true for the people of the Columbia River and Great Basin when they were moved to the Warm Springs Reservation. With the disruption of seasonal cycles and well-established trade patterns, the whole rhythm and momentum of their culture was broken. And behind the cultural turmoil was the more basic problem of physical survival. ☐ Life for the new inhabitants of the Warm Springs Reservation became characterized by poverty and a sedentary non-productivity. People accustomed to wresting a living from the earth became dependent on barrels of flour, sugar, and crackers distributed from the commissary at the Warm Springs Agency. Poignant stories are still told about people's great-grandparents trying to make a palatable gravy or bread out of crushed pilot crackers, or fearing corn kernels because they looked too much like the teeth of old people. And often there was not enough of these foods. ☐ While it is unlikely that the U.S. Government intended for the people of Warm Springs to starve, it is clear from the provisions of the Treaty of 1855 that the tribes were to be utterly dependent on the government until such time as they were "civilized," i.e., schooled in the economic and social patterns of the white culture. In Article 2 of the treaty, which details how the one hundred fifty thousand dollars in payments were to be spent, the government's intentions are apparent.

The Warm Springs Agency at the turn of the century was dominated by the boarding school (top center) and the Presbyterian Church. Only the commissary (third building from right) still stands. (Moorhouse Collection, University of Oregon Library)

All of which several sums of money shall be expended for the use and benefit of the confederated bands, under the direction of the President of the United States, who may from time to time, at his discretion determine what proportion thereof shall be expended for such objects as in his judgment will promote their well-being and advance them in civilization; for their moral improvement and education, for building, opening and fencing farms, breaking land, providing teams, stock, agricultural implements, seeds, &c; for clothing, provisions and tools; for medical purposes, providing mechanics and farmers, and for arms and ammunition.*

Warm Springs was to be a quiet little farming community, though only a small number of Wascos had ever cultivated land before the treaty. All across the nation, Indians who had never farmed were being wooed with plows and plots of land. As Secretary of the Interior A.H.H. Stuart recommended in his 1851 annual report, ". . . to tame a savage, one must tie him down to the soil."† Frustrated government employees wondered why Indians showed little interest. In Warm Springs, as on many other reservations, poor soil, inadequate water, a short growing season, and delayed shipments of tools made agriculture an unattractive alternative. Tilling the land was an alien notion to a people who were accustomed to the earth annually providing all the food they needed, and planted fields

---

*The text of the Treaty with the Tribes of Middle Oregon, 1855, is printed in Charles J. Kappler (ed.), *Indian Affairs: Laws and Treaties,* Vol. II (Treaties).

†Thelma Drake Cliff used this quote in her 1942 master's thesis, "A History of the Warm Springs Reservation, 1855–1900."

were often left untended when the salmon runs were peaking in the Columbia. Still, Agent John Smith cheerfully reported in 1881 that "scarcely an Indian family upon this reservation can be found that does not have a patch of ground in cultivation." Judging by the childhood memories of today's older people, farming was quite common in the first half of this century, despite the odds against real profits. Now, fewer than three thousand acres are under cultivation, mostly to supply feed for cattle and horses.

True to the treaty, wood frame buildings began sprouting in the 1860s on the barren bench above Shitike Creek at the Agency. By 1862 there were seven promised buildings, but so hastily and crudely were they built that only three—the sawmill, flouring mill, and the wagon and plow shop—were fit for use. The others—the blacksmith and gunsmith shops, the schoolhouse and the hospital—were either unfinished or ill-equipped. Inadequate supplies and jerry-built structures continued to be a problem through the century, creating a rather poor model of civilization for the "savages" and undermining the efforts of reservation personnel during a critical period of economic transition. Asking the Indians to give up their old ways without presenting reasonable alternatives was a sure way to foster unhealthy dependence, a habit that later became extremely hard to break.

Ideally, the Warm Springs people were to learn trades and an Anglo style of survival skills so they might support themselves when government assistance was withdrawn after a period of twenty years. But living residents can recall working in the shops and at the dairy farm as part of their boarding school curriculum well into the twentieth century. It is safe to say that the idea of entrepreneurism did not catch on as agents had hoped. Some of the skills were taken back to home and farm, but most families were not able to survive without the government rations. Even those with cattle, sheep, hay, and grain to sell often relied on their handmade buckskin gloves, dried salmon, or animal pelts to bring them cash for staple foods. Odd jobs doing seasonal farm work, hauling goods, or helping in cattle round-ups were other sources of income.

While the people waited for the highly touted benefits of civilization, their traditional methods of providing for themselves were fast eroding. They sank further into poverty and dependence. In the early years, many families frequently exercised their off-reservation fishing rights, usually spending the salmon harvesting months on the Columbia and only wintering on the reservation, much to the exasperation of school superintendents and agricultural personnel. But their off-reservation rights were not always honored. In an 1890 letter to Washington, D.C., reservation agent J.C. Luckey reported:

> The Indians were all but famishing. They raised no crops last year (weather prevented it), and had no supplies of fish, game to subsist upon; during the later winter months. The game is nearly all killed off and they were more than ever before denied the right to take salmon last summer at the Columbia River.*

Apparently, non-Indians in the ceded area had objected to the traffic of Indians off the reservation, and when fences and warnings failed to keep hunting and gathering parties off their land and fishermen away from the river, they pressed for a second treaty. The so-called Treaty of 1865 was signed by a handful of Indians who agreed to give up all the tribes' hunting, fishing and gathering rights in the ceded area and to submit to a pass system for leaving the reservation—all for the paltry sum of thirty-five hundred dollars, which was to be spent on agricultural tools and supplies. This treaty was never fully enforced and was repeatedly discredited in court decisions until it was finally pronounced dead by a federal judge in 1969. It may have been bogus, but the Treaty of 1865 was an accurate measure of the feelings harbored by settlers who made it increasingly difficult for their roaming neighbors to gain access to their traditional sites. While

---

* A photocopy of this letter is in the possession of the Confederated Tribes.

134

the off-reservation rights are still valid today, they are sometimes moot in the face of barbed wire, gates, dams, and poor salmon runs.

The first eighty years on the reservation were permeated by a profound sense of powerlessness, which is arguably more destructive in the long run than physical deprivation. The old people today talk almost proudly about the days when "nobody had nothing" and everyone was equally poor. Simple things like healthy babies, weekend-long card games, and laundry days at the hot springs glittered against the bleak backdrop of food shortages, disease, and patched moccasins wrapped in flour sacks and baling wire. Those were the days when the cattle were properly cared for, the children were still in awe of the whipman, and the elders expected silence when they spoke.

What the old people find more difficult to describe is the pervasive shadow cast by the government's presence on the reservation. The people's future had been taken out of their own hands and entrusted to a distant government whose local representatives—the fatherly reservation agent and his cadre of schoolteachers and technical personnel—had almost unlimited authority over the people's lives. If early communications between the Agency and Washington, D.C. are any indication, the officials themselves must have felt some of the same powerlessness as they begged their superiors for the food and money which was their stock in trade.

It was not just the slow bureaucratic workings of a faraway White Father that kept the reservation people hungry and their natural initiative stifled. Government policy was founded on the expectation that Indians would eventually exist only as individuals, not as tribes, and that reservations would be but a temporary solution to the "Indian problem." The government was so busy trying to make independent tradesmen and farmers of a basically communal people that it failed to explore ways in which tribal economies could be developed. One of the most destructive actions the government could take was to undermine the land base that promised to be the tribes' greatest economic asset. But it did just that.

Late in the nineteenth century, the interests of social reformers and the land-hungry coincided long enough to produce a piece of legislation that had devastating effects on reservation land holdings across the country. The Dawes Severalty Act of 1887 was, nominally, an effort to assimilate Indians into the cultural mainstream by encouraging a proprietary interest in their land. Private land ownership, a hallmark of "civilization," was felt to be the key to the transformation of reservation Indians into modern, productive citizens.

Under the Dawes Act, reservations were carved into 160-, 80-, and 40-acre parcels, which were allotted to individual Indians and held in trust by the government for a period of twenty-five years, after which time full title could be transferred to the allottees unless they were deemed incompetent. Surplus land could be purchased by the government, with interest on the receipts to be spent on the education and civilization of the tribes. Further, citizenship would be conferred on allottees who showed signs of giving up their tribal ways. Despite its apparent intent, the Dawes Act actually played into the hands of non-Indian settlers and removed millions of acres of reservation land from tribal ownership. Not only did "surplus" land become available for settlement after the allotments were made, but when Indian owners acquired title years later and were faced with taxes, they often sold their allotments to eager non-Indians, thus alienating former tribal lands. It is estimated that between 1886 and 1934, ninety million acres of reservation land were lost nationwide because of this legislation, a tragic sixty-five percent reduction of a land base that was already a fraction of the aboriginal territories.

Some of Warm Springs' neighbors suffered greatly from the Dawes Act. The Grand Ronde and Siletz reservations on the Oregon coast virtually disappeared. The Umatilla Reservation in eastern Oregon and the Yakima Reservation in south central Washington became checkerboards of tribal and alienated land, creating jurisdictional confusion and making economic development difficult. The Warm Springs Reservation fared much better. About one-fifth of the reservation was allotted, but most of the parcels were never taken

out of trust status and therefore little was alienated. Warm Springs was also fortunate in that unallotted land was not purchased by the government and the original boundaries remained intact. One of the outcomes of allotment that has been a problem at Warm Springs, however, is the shared ownership of a parcel by numerous descendants of the original allottee, pitting relatives against one another and making each section impossible to use.

Allotment came to an end with the Indian Reorganization Act of 1934, a wide-ranging reform measure that in part provided for the tribal buy-back of allotted lands. Tribal purchases at Warm Springs have reduced allotments to ten percent of the reservation, with only one percent of the land alienated. Today, tribal members may use tribal lands for home sites, agriculture, or industry through a system of lifetime assignments or short- and long-term leases approved by Tribal Council. The determination of tribal leaders to keep tribal land holdings intact and in trust for the benefit of all members, as frustrating as it may be for enterprising individuals, has resulted in a particularly strong land base which translates into both economic and political strength for the Tribes.

NEW POWER, NEW WAYS

Through years of fumbling U.S. policy, when the only certainty in Indian country was the growth and entrenchment of the federal bureaucracy overseeing it, the people of Warm Springs simply concentrated on surviving as individuals and as a community. Their numbers slowly increased, despite deadly epidemics and the disruption of family life caused by the boarding schools. And, somehow, when it came time for power to be returned to them, they had the strength to receive it.

The Depression years brought no special suffering to the reservation; in fact, the 1930s brought new opportunities, not the least of which were the Civilian Conservation Corps (CCC) camps on the reservation that provided jobs where there had been none. Also, in the spirit of Roosevelt's New Deal, Indians across the country were given a way out of the dependence and paralysis that had developed from the government's misguided and futile assimilation efforts. The Indian Reorganization (or Wheeler-Howard) Act of 1934, a direct if belated response to the failure of unilateral policy-making, recognized tribal integrity not only by putting an end to land allotment but also by encouraging tribes to govern their own affairs.

Beyond the provisions for tribal self-government, the Wheeler-Howard Act allowed for the incorporation of tribes as business entities. Warm Springs hastened to take advantage of this by drawing up and approving a corporate charter in 1938, two months after their constitution was in place. The charter gave the Confederated Tribes all the privileges, powers, and immunities of a federal corporation while designating tribal members as shareholders. The secretary-treasurer of the newly established Tribal Council minded the young corporation, a job that grew more and more removed from the Council until the 1970s, when the position came to be known as general manager. The Tribes' effort to separate business and political functions, while not always clearly defined, has been a source of strength and stability for the Tribes.

With sound political and economic machinery in place, and the BIA's role redefined as more advisory than authoritarian, Warm Springs was ready to plan its own future. The development that took place in the next forty-five years surpassed anyone's expectations. It was a dizzying spiral of growth that showed no signs of slowing until the recession of the early 1980s. But it started slowly, and the Tribes had to suffer the huge cultural loss of Celilo Falls before business would begin booming.

The new tribal corporation had no income of its own, but a handful of employees under contract with the federal government helped to administer BIA program monies and a revolving credit fund set up under the reorganization act. The first telephone operator, who retired from a tribal management position in 1980, remembered that in 1938 "the phone didn't ring much," so she spent her time on such tasks as typing up milk bills for the tribal dairy and purchasing equip-

ment for the blacksmith. One of the employment benefits at the time was first pick of the tribal farm's pig slaughter, she noted.

World War II was a boon to the Tribes, as it was for a whole nation weary of the Great Depression. While many Warm Springs men volunteered for military service, the Tribes helped fill the wartime demand for lumber by signing their first timber contract in 1942. The BIA had been cutting and milling timber since the previous century, but only enough to supply the reservation's construction needs. With a steady source of income expected from timber sales, the Tribes confidently initiated per capita payments to its members, a practice that continues today. Each member now receives one hundred dollars a month and a year-end bonus of as much as fifteen hundred dollars if business has been good or year-end tribal assets can justify it. For members under eighteen, the monthly per capitas are placed in Individual Indian Monies accounts with the BIA. These "trust funds" are made available on the eighteenth and twenty-first birthdays, theoretically to pay college expenses.

The completion of U.S. Highway 26 through the reservation in 1949 prepared the community logistically and psychologically for the development to come. Always isolated from the rest of Oregon, Warm Springs suddenly felt the very direct influence of the white world, as a steady stream of truckers and tourists passed through on trips between Portland and points east, and tribal members could more easily leave the reservation for shopping and entertainment. The highway also connected Warm Springs to the rest of the state commercially, making tribal business ventures more feasible.

Meanwhile, the federal government was making its presence felt once again with a new set of policies designed to make reservations obsolete. During the 1950s, the termination policy "liberated" a great number of successful reservations, including three in Oregon, that were judged to be ready to exist without government support. At the same time, promising young reservation Indians were being given one-way tickets to distant urban areas for career and training

opportunities unavailable on their reservations. The intention of this "relocation" program was not to bring trained, experienced people back to the reservations but to remove them permanently; participants were asked to sell their belongings before leaving. About a dozen men and women from Warm Springs participated, moving as far as Texas in one case, but the government "failed" with every one of them; all the relocated individuals came home, some to careers with the burgeoning tribal organization and some to the same situations they had left. The policies of relocation and termination put tribes in double jeopardy: being economically underdeveloped might mean losing talented individuals, but being too successful might mean losing the reservation. Warm Springs was determined to take matters into its own hands.

The real turning point in the reservation's economic picture did not come until the fishing grounds at Celilo Falls were inundated by The Dalles Dam in 1957. The destruction of an important source of income and subsistence forced the Tribes to consider economic alternatives. And while they knew that no price tag could be affixed to the loss, the four million dollars the Tribes received as compensation from the U.S. Corps of Engineers created a singular opportunity for investment and enterprise.

Tribal leaders embraced that opportunity. Though it was common for Indian claims and settlements to be parceled out to tribal members on a per capita basis, the Confederated Tribes took a different tack. After numerous community meetings, Tribal Council decided to distribute only a small portion of the settlement (five hundred dollars to each member) and to bank the rest. Almost immediately, the Tribes earmarked one hundred thousand dollars for a comprehensive survey of the reservation's natural and human resources. The five-volume document produced by Oregon State College (now University) researchers in 1960 has proved invaluable to tribal planners through the years, even providing good reference material twenty years later when the Tribes were formulating their second major community development plan. Pointing to timber and recreation as the keys to res-

ervation economic development, the survey also determined through extensive interviews that tribal members desired more jobs, greater educational opportunities, and the higher standard of living that would result.

The series of Tribal Councils guiding the reservation through this critical period were the usual mix of young and old, ranchers and retirees, chiefs and laymen. Most had not finished high school but they were able to combine what their elders had taught them with good instincts and unflagging energy to produce intelligent consensus time and time again. One of their fellow members, not satisfied with his high school diploma, took educational leave and went off to the University of Oregon with his young family. Vernon Jackson returned to the reservation in 1958 with the Tribes' first college degree. Already a legend in tribal history, Jackson was probably the reservation's first "workaholic." As secretary-treasurer of the Council until his sudden death in 1969, Jackson brought a worldly perspective and a limitless imagination to his management of the tribal corporation. His accomplishments were not single-handed, but the developments of the 1960s certainly bore Jackson's mark.

While the Tribes were awakening to the great potential of their reservation resources, an income opportunity arose on the Deschutes River where Portland General Electric (PGE) was laying plans for the construction of two hydroelectric projects. Since the Treaty of 1855 defined boundaries that ran down the middle of the Deschutes and Metolius River channels, it was clear that the utility would have to gain the cooperation of the Confederated Tribes in order to start building. Not only did the Tribes claim half the riverbed, but they argued that half the water's power potential was theirs, too. It was a landmark example of the Tribes negotiating as equals with a corporate neighbor, establishing the reservation as a political and economic entity and the Tribes as a private landowner with rights to its water. It proved to be a lucrative, if not always easy, source of income.

Negotiations for Pelton Dam, several miles upriver from Warm Springs, resulted in a 1955 rental agreement compensating the Tribes with a fixed annual fee

for twenty years, at which time the fee could be renegotiated with adjustments every ten years thereafter. A similar agreement was made in 1961 for Round Butte Dam, a few miles farther upstream, with adjustments ten years after completion of the dam and every five years thereafter. Combined income from the dams in 1965 was three hundred thousand dollars. In 1977, when arbitrators approved a more favorable rent formula, the rent on Round Butte alone jumped to just over one million dollars (retroactive to 1974). But PGE would not sit still for an arbitrated rent hike of four hundred fifty percent in 1982, and no money changed hands until 1984 when a federal court judge reduced the back rent due and set the 1985 rate at six million dollars, with annual adjustments through the year 2001 tied to the changing consumer price index.

One of the most impressive facts about the PGE agreements was the clause in the Pelton contract that reserved the right of the Tribes to install a generator at the reregulating dam downstream from the main dam. Three decades later, the Tribes threw the switch on their own hydroelectric project.

The Oregon State study had drawn the Tribes' attention to the economic potential of another reservation river. Surely tourism could grow along the banks of the beautiful Warm Springs River, whose hot mineral springs, colorful canyon, and clean waters were already legendary. Land around the springs that once belonged to a woman named Xnita had been sold years before to a non-Indian doctor who had built a small spa. In 1961, the Tribes bought back the alienated land for one hundred sixty-five thousand dollars and breathed life back into the run-down spa. Capitalizing on the restorative spring waters that had soothed Xnita and her ancestors, the Tribes soon built the Olympic-sized pool, rental cottages, guest tepees, restaurant, and miniature golf course that are Kah-Nee-Ta Village. A flood in 1964 swept away the bridge over the river and a few never-occupied cottages, but, undaunted, the Tribes rebuilt.

Then in 1971, with low-interest loans from the federal Economic Development Administration (EDA), the Tribes began construction of Kah-Nee-Ta Lodge up the road, in the hope of attracting convention busi-

ness. It was one of a dozen EDA-funded resorts built on Indian reservations in the 1970s, about half of which are viable businesses today. The beautiful contemporary cedar lodge on a bluff overlooking the Warm Springs River valley is a tribal showpiece but somewhat of a financial burden. Summers bring tourists streaming over the Cascade Mountains to fill the Village and Lodge, but the off-season is eerily quiet, a time when locals find themselves virtually alone at what feels like a private, very exclusive country club. In 1983, the EDA began sending threatening letters to the Tribes about "long overdue" payments on the loans, but the Tribes successfully argued that payments were to be made from resort profits—and Kah-Nee-Ta had not yet shown a profit.

Hardly a neutral word has been spoken about Kah-Nee-Ta since it was built; the reservation community has always been divided over whether it was an appropriate project. One of the arguments in its favor was that it would provide jobs for locals, but tribal members now comprise less than a quarter of the Kah-Nee-Ta payroll, and visitors express disappointment when they have little or no contact with Indians. The naming of a tribal member as manager in the late 1970s and the creation of a board of directors separate from the Tribal Council have been attempts to stabilize and de-politicize resort management and address tribal members' concerns. Then came the era of "Kah-Nee-Ta, not just another resort, another culture," an effort to make the reservation people and culture more visible. An "Indianized" menu, traditional outdoor salmon bakes put on by reservation women, more local artwork in the gift shops, crafts demonstrations, and historical displays produced an Indian presence at the resort. Renewed interest was sparked in Kah-Nee-Ta's management training program for tribal members, and in 1982, the resort finally broke even for the first time. But it was a short-lived turnaround and, by 1986, the difficulty of delivering on the promise of "another culture" had caused the board to opt for de-Indianization and to return to promoting Kah-Nee-Ta as a spa.

As when Lewis and Clark were extended hospitality by the river people, the Tribes today encourage visitors to come to their reservation. An information center and gift shop at the eastern entry welcomes tourists and offers them beadwork, travel advice, and inexpensive cigarettes. Fishermen are allowed to drop their lines into a few select spots in reservation rivers and lakes. The public is invited to respectfully attend powwows and celebrations—if they want to risk being asked to sit apart from the Indians during a feast or to circle up for a tongue-in-cheek "honky dance" at a powwow. There are limits to their hospitality, as shown by the community's ambiguous feelings about Kah-Nee-Ta. When a ski resort on the pristine slopes of Mt. Jefferson was proposed by tribal planners in the early 1970s, tribal members voiced a loud and clear "no." Tourism as an income-producing industry on the reservation clearly has yet to live up to the potential noted in the OSU study.

BOARDS AS BREAD AND BUTTER

Timber had been a lively and important part of reservation life since the days of logging with horses. Small BIA sawmills operated for a time among the trees, with tiny settlements growing up around them. But improved roads made the transport of logs to a central location more economical, and the mills were reduced to heaps of weathered boards. By the early 1940s, most of the trees sold by the Tribes were being processed at a mill built and owned by non-Indians just outside the Agency.

The OSU study had indicated that the Tribes would benefit greatly by being both owner and processor of their timber. In 1967, after dismissing the idea of building a brand new wood products complex, the Tribes borrowed capital to purchase the mill at Warm Springs and the related plywood plant in Madras, establishing the tribal enterprise known as "Warm Springs Forest Products Industries (WSFPI)." The new owners, with the help of existing management, were turning a profit within the year. They soon added a stud mill and veneer plant to diversify their operations, and in a multi-million dollar renovation a decade later, they moved the plywood plant to Warm Springs and automated it, and brought the whole operation up to industry standards. Then the recession hit, and from a profit of four

Tribal members like Julian Smith, who pulls lumber on the sawmill green chain, make a good living at Warm Springs Forest Products Industries, one of Jefferson County's biggest employers. (Cynthia D. Stowell)

million dollars in 1978, figures tumbled into the red in 1982. But the mill survived the down market with its work force intact, helping to buoy not only the reservation's but Jefferson County's economy, too. With their "Plan for the Eighties," WSFPI and the Tribes have tried to prepare for good and bad times alike by discussing the redesign of their facilities to match the smaller trees that now predominate in the tribal forest and by considering products beyond the lumber, studs,

veneer, plywood, and chips that have been WSFPI's standard products.

The mill—and the timber it buys, the people it employs, and the contractors it supports—is the reservation's biggest and most successful enterprise. Under the guidance of a board of directors composed of both tribal members and non-Indians, WSFPI has the combined goals of employing tribal members and making a profit. Today, about half the three hundred WSFPI em-

ployees are tribal members, married to members, or Indians affiliated with other tribes. The mill manager is a tribal member, as are other key managers. And employment ripples extend to a dozen tribal member contractors and their crews, who harvest eighty-five percent of the annual cut of eighty-one million board feet. "Working in the woods" is popular with Warm Springs men, but with logging restricted to a seven-month season, job opportunities in the forest are usually saturated.

All tribal members benefit from the mill's profits, a portion of which goes into the tribal treasury for reservation programs and "shareholder dividends." But the Tribes' real bread and butter comes from the stumpage fees (the cost of timber as it stands in the forest) paid by the mill, which soared as high as eleven-and-a-half million dollars in 1979. As trustee, the federal government takes ten percent off the top of tribal profits, but these "administrative fees" are returned to the Tribes to fund such forest enhancement programs as thinning and slash removal.

While the Tribes own and exploit their timber, responsibility for managing the forest in the interest of the Tribes lies with the BIA. To that end, the Bureau maintains a forestry staff on the reservation to keep a current forest inventory, lay out sales, rehabilitate the forest after cutting, and provide fire protection. The Bureau of Indian Affairs also determines the annual allowable cut, based on sustained yield harvesting. In the late 1970s, the Tribes threatened to sue the U.S. Government for mismanagement of the forest, charging that antiquated and inaccurate inventory methods were being used to calculate the annual cut figure. Tribal decision-makers felt the harvest was not keeping pace with the natural loss of old, first-growth timber, and that the Tribes could realize much more income if the annual cut were increased. The Bureau of Indian Affairs has since improved its inventory methods and, although the annual allowable cut (which was already at a somewhat accelerated level) has not been increased, BIA foresters are working more closely with the Tribes in planning harvests.

Tribal members often express the fear that their forest resource is being depleted and that their children's children may not be able to depend on stumpage fees as an income base. Managers and members agree, however, that it is dangerous for the Tribes to rely too heavily on one source of income. In an effort to diversify, as well as to create more jobs, the Tribes have launched a number of smaller enterprises, including an electronics sub-assembly plant (which closed in 1985 for lack of contracts), tribal garage and vehicle pool, information center and gift shop, construction office, and credit program. In 1986, tribal members voted to appropriate three hundred thousand dollars for the establishment of a small garment manufacturing plant; by year-end, Warm Springs Apparel Industries was taking orders for car covers and sportswear.

By far the most ambitious and successful of the newer enterprises has been the thirty million dollar hydroelectric plant installed in the Pelton Reregulating Dam in 1982. Warm Springs Power Enterprises produces an average of eight million kilowatts of electricity a month, most of which it sells to Pacific Power and Light. Income has exceeded the Tribes' own forecasts, putting them ahead of schedule in repaying the federal and state loans that supplemented tribal funds in construction of the first federally licensed hydroelectric plant owned by an Indian tribe.

In 1986, the Tribes went into the broadcasting business when 100,000-watt KWSI Radio began sending signals throughout central Oregon. Started with tribal dollars and a BIA economic development grant as a profit-making venture, the Kah-Nee-Ta-based FM station has also provided jobs and training for five tribal members, including four disc jockeys and one salesperson. Its Top Forty music format was later supplemented by the more culturally oriented KWSO, a low-watt educational station funded with a federal grant and, eventually, with profits from the commercial station.

STEWARDS OF THE LAND

More than many other tribes, the Columbia River people had a highly developed commercial component to their culture, which no doubt predisposed them to successfully exploiting their new homeland.

141

But this exploitation, along with the legalistic relationship with the land that grew out of the treaty, has assigned a material importance to the reservation land that is very different from the people's traditional view of the earth.

Consequently, the Warm Springs people today are faced with some difficult land-use issues, an ironic turn of events for a culture lauded for its harmonious coexistence with the natural world. There is an ambivalence reflected in the fact that the reservation is not the people's original homeland and in the feeling "This is all we have left—let's take care of it."

Fortunately, tribal leaders have had a strong instinct for preservation, even when it has meant temporarily losing favor with the membership. It is no accident that the Warm Springs Reservation has stayed relatively intact, and has grown, through decades that have seen severe land losses on other reservations.

One of their first fights over the land base also turned out to be the most protracted, taking more than a hundred years to resolve. The first survey of the reservation was done by a man named Handley in 1871 without the benefit of Supt. Joel Palmer's map, which was attached to the treaty in Washington, D.C. The tribes never believed that the northern boundary was drawn correctly, and a second survey done in 1887 by John McQuinn disputed Handley's line. Generations of tribal leaders fought for the land between the two lines, while white settlers carved out homesteads and sheep ranches and the government established a National Forest in the disputed area. Finally in 1972, the persistence of the Tribes and their lawyers was rewarded with Public Law 92-427, which acknowledged the McQuinn line and added two wedge-shaped pieces of mostly timbered land to the north and west boundaries, expanding the reservation by 61,000 acres. The McQuinn Act phases in tribal ownership over a twenty-year period, and by 1992 the Confederated Tribes will be free to harvest and process timber from the McQuinn Strip.

In recent years, the joint Tribal and BIA realty office has started making purchases outside the boundaries of the reservation in the ceded area. The first such transaction was in 1977, when the Tribes bought an eight-acre parcel in nearby Madras in order to build a loading dock for their lumber. In 1982, they purchased 304 acres of fertile farmland on the east side of the Deschutes River, as a possible site for employee housing; it is currently leased by tribal members for livestock grazing. Then, in 1979, the Tribes bought back an important cultural site—888 acres at the Sherars Bridge, or Sherars Falls, section of the Deschutes River, north of the reservation, where the Tygh and other Indians have trapped and netted salmon and steelhead for thousands of years.

Surrounding governments have watched the Tribes' acquisitions with some trepidation, concerned that valuable pieces of land would be taken off the tax rolls. While two of the three purchases have been placed in trust with the U.S. Government, the loss in taxes has been minimal because of the low assessed value of the land. Non-Indian fishermen at Sherars Bridge also predicted that they would lose access to their favorite holes after tribal purchase, but except for one conservation closure that forced Indians to put away their nets, too, the Tribes have allowed non-Indians to continue fishing.

All too often in Indian country, land has come to be equated with money. In the years since the treaties, tribes have tried to reclaim lands they felt they had lost unfairly, but with subsequent settlement of these lands by non-Indians, the most they could usually hope for was financial reparation. The Indian Claims Commission was set up in 1946 to hear such claims, and Warm Springs was among the many tribes to take advantage of this legal avenue.

In their 1951 claim, the Tribes maintained that the land they had ceded in the 1855 treaty amounted to ten million acres and that the value of one acre at that time was one dollar. Figuring they had received two hundred thousand dollars in "treaty considerations," they were claiming the balance of 9.8 million dollars. In the next twenty years, the U.S. whittled this amount down to 1.2 million dollars based on how much of the ten million acres was used exclusively by the treaty-signers' ancestors and how much money had been

spent by the government since the treaty in services to Warm Springs ("offsets"). Tribal voters approved this settlement in 1973, but it would be twelve years before the payment was distributed to tribal members; the Tribes first had to determine who was eligible to participate, based on prior participation in other claims. Meanwhile, accrued interest had swelled the amount to 3.3 million dollars.

It is not just their land that the Tribes have worked hard to protect and enhance. They have also been vigilant in protecting their rights to the water flowing through or bordering the reservation. In the 1970s, as Americans began to see clearly the limits of natural resources that had been taken for granted for centuries, pressure came to bear on Indian reservations and their unused potential. President Carter's water policy and legislative bills introduced around the same time proposed limiting Indian's future rights to only that water currently being used. In 1979, plans for a much needed domestic water system at Warm Springs to replace the old, inadequate BIA system were hurried to tribal referendum and voters approved the eight million dollar project. It puzzled some people that water would be drawn from the Deschutes instead of the more pristine Shitike Creek. But tribal leaders will quietly admit their sense of urgency in establishing firm rights to the water of that boundary river.

The Tribal Council has had to take some strong stands on resource management to preserve the quality of the reservation land base. For a people accustomed to limitless land and plentiful resources, the need for conservation on their circumscribed piece of land has been hard to accept. Deer have been over-hunted and the grasslands overgrazed; streamsides are littered; hillsides are torn up by off-road vehicles.

"This is my land," says the individual tribal member. "I have treaty rights and I can do whatever I want with it." But the Warm Springs Tribal Council has responded with closures or new regulations, continuing to operate on the premise that treaty rights to the land are tribal, not individual, rights.

Indian ranchers, hunters, and fishermen are an in-dependent lot, resistent to regulation. But in the early 1980s, Council found it necessary to place limitations on all three. The Sherars closure during the first summer of tribal ownership left some fishermen feeling betrayed, but the fishery re-opened the next year because of improved salmon and steelhead returns. Deer hunting on the reservation was prohibited during 1984 after a head count revealed severely depleted herds. When hunting was reinstated in 1985, it was much reduced, from one deer per family per month year-round to the same monthly quota for a three-month period only.

Management of the range has been particularly difficult because of the many private interests involved and the use of both tribal and allotted lands for grazing horses and cattle. But in 1985 the Council ended years of anarchy on the range by adopting a new management ordinance and pledging to work with the BIA and OSU Extension Service on solving the problems of overgrazing and livestock control. Livestock owners will now have to work together in grazing groups to adopt methods that will conserve the resource for the continued economic benefit of all ranchers.

Now and then, tribal members are the ones to blow the whistle on resource exploitation, particularly when it comes to the timber. For example, in 1984, when the BIA proposed timber sales from an aesthetically and culturally sensitive area of virgin growth in a pristine river canyon, tribal members objected. They were joined by the conservation concerns of the tribal natural resources department. One outcome was the shelving of the sales; another was pressure to formulate a tribal Watershed Management Plan; but a third, less tangible, result was an improvement in the sharing of information and an acknowledgment that non-economic concerns are valid in making decisions about the forest.

At one time, such cooperation and balance was a natural part of their culture; now it takes thousands of dollars, years of research by numerous committees and departments, and much dialogue to ensure that the land is used wisely.

ALL FOR THE PEOPLE

When the Tribes made it their first priority to develop the reservation's natural resources in the early 1960s, it was for the expressed purpose of raising the people's standard of living. The assumption was that development would bring jobs and services; jobs would bring prosperity and confidence; and the Tribes would then be free to turn their attention to social and cultural problems, if they still existed—a kind of "trickle-down" theory of social improvement.

In the meantime, Warm Springs in the 1960s and 1970s could best be described as a boomtown. Everything the Confederated Tribes touched seemed to turn to gold (even Kah-Nee-Ta was valuable for public relations), and there appeared to be no end to tribal growth and prosperity. By the end of the 1970s, the Tribes' annual revenues had grown to around twenty million dollars, with the annual tribal operating budget around ten million dollars. A huge administrative structure employing nearly four hundred people had developed to run the tribal corporation and to provide community services to tribal members. Six hundred more were employed by Kah-Nee-Ta and WSFPI, and another four hundred in federal, private, and seasonal employment. The reservation had become the largest employer in central Oregon, with about half the jobs held by tribal members, spouses of tribal members, or Indians of other tribes.

Money flowed freely as the Tribes tried to shout down the specter of poverty that had haunted them since they moved to the reservation. Per capitas and year-end bonuses in addition to salaries helped push family incomes above the national average. There was opportunity where there had once been hopelessness, and waves of optimism washed over the community. Elected and appointed leaders traveled often on generous expense accounts to convene with other tribes, to lobby in Washington, D.C., or to otherwise nurture relations with Indian and non-Indian governments alike. Warm Springs quietly but powerfully established itself as a model of success among reservations nationwide.

The face of Warm Springs seemed to change overnight as tribal assets went to work on community improvements. Planners were hired and a community development plan was drawn up. Architects from Portland sketched out their visions for the community's growth, while tribal members blinked with disbelief at scale drawings of the tract homes, apartments, and playgrounds of the future. After more than half the dwellings on the reservation were classified as substandard in 1965, the people voted to appropriate one million dollars in tribal funds to build new homes and to set up a tribal credit program to assist members with home purchases. They ambivalently said good-bye to the humble collections of old barracks that had been hauled down from the Madras Air Base after the war to become the neighborhoods of Hollywood and Greensville, and to the rough-hewn farmhouses their parents and grandparents had built from reservation timber. In 1969, the first loop of the West Hills subdivision was built. Soon after, trailer sites were carved into another hillside. Generations of families long crowded into tiny homes could now begin to stretch out a little, and people scattered in the rural areas could move into a more central location.

During the 1970s, three more loops were added to West Hills, much of it subsidized by the Federal Department of Housing and Urban Development (HUD), but the waiting list seemed to grow longer. Housing spilled out into the rich farmland of the Tenino Valley, with rental townhouses and duplexes rising out of a pasture behind the rodeo grounds and low density housing dotting a nearby bench. Senior citizens were given a commanding view of the community from a new complex of homes and a social center built for them by the Tribes.

Public buildings also changed the profile of Warm Springs. A community center with gym and meeting rooms was built on the site of the old government dairy farm. Nearby, a sleek cedar and glass administration building consolidated tribal and BIA departments and the Tribal Council, giving the Tribes a polished, professional look. An industrial park took over a meadow along the road to Kah-Nee-Ta, housing the BIA's fire control agency, an electronics sub-assembly plant, the tribal motor pool, and warehouses. A new

144

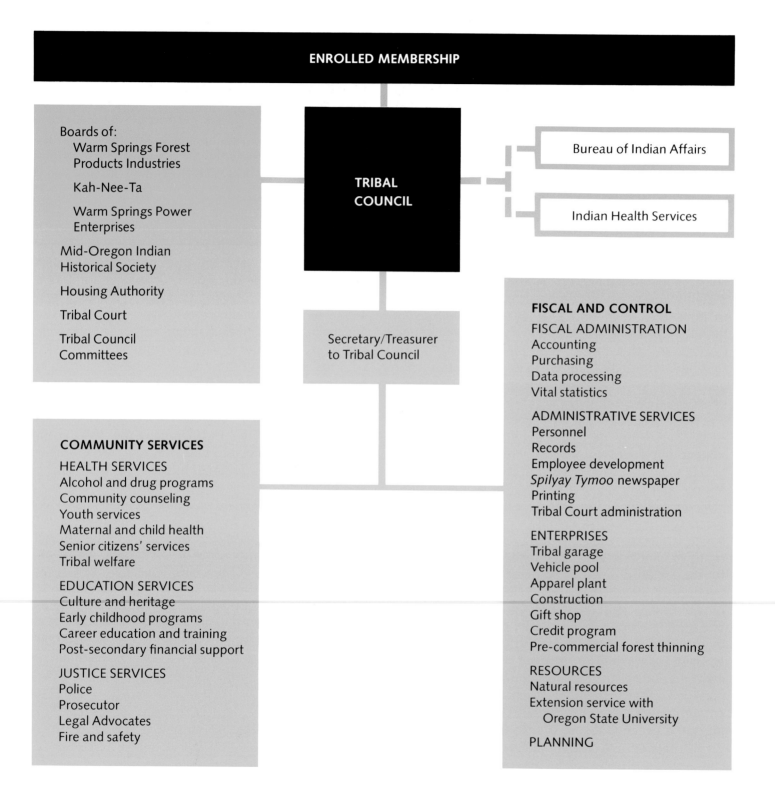

ENROLLED MEMBERSHIP

Boards of:
Warm Springs Forest
Products Industries

Kah-Nee-Ta

Warm Springs Power
Enterprises

Mid-Oregon Indian
Historical Society

Housing Authority

Tribal Court

Tribal Council
Committees

TRIBAL COUNCIL

Bureau of Indian Affairs

Indian Health Services

Secretary/Treasurer
to Tribal Council

COMMUNITY SERVICES

HEALTH SERVICES
Alcohol and drug programs
Community counseling
Youth services
Maternal and child health
Senior citizens' services
Tribal welfare

EDUCATION SERVICES
Culture and heritage
Early childhood programs
Career education and training
Post-secondary financial support

JUSTICE SERVICES
Police
Prosecutor
Legal Advocates
Fire and safety

FISCAL AND CONTROL

FISCAL ADMINISTRATION
Accounting
Purchasing
Data processing
Vital statistics

ADMINISTRATIVE SERVICES
Personnel
Records
Employee development
Spilyay Tymoo newspaper
Printing
Tribal Court administration

ENTERPRISES
Tribal garage
Vehicle pool
Apparel plant
Construction
Gift shop
Credit program
Pre-commercial forest thinning

RESOURCES
Natural resources
Extension service with
Oregon State University

PLANNING

145

tribal service station replaced another dairy barn. Longhouses built in the 1960s to replace makeshift plywood and canvas structures were expanded and bathrooms brought indoors. Plans were in the offing for a shopping center, an airport, a community learning center, a justice facility, and on and on.

But something happened at the end of the 1970s. People started saying "no" to the architects' drawings presented at general council meetings and for referendum votes. They began to look at the quality of programs rather than the facilities proposed to house them. As West Hills became shabby, tribal members tried to convince their planners that the congestion of tract living was not attractive and the flimsiness of HUD construction would not do. By the 1980s, settlement patterns were reversing, and people began to get loans to build their own homes away from the Agency. Instead of planning and building whole new neighborhoods, the Tribes concentrated on developing homesites and eventually started their own construction department for tribal members who didn't want to use off-reservation contractors.

The recession of the early 1980s forced the slowdown that many tribal members had been secretly hoping. But it was not an easy time for the Tribes, as WSFPI's profits evaporated, federal dollars were drying up, and difficult decisions had to be made about program priorities. The necessary budget cuts were a meaningful exercise in identifying waste and excess. At the same time, the vulnerability of the timber industry to economic downturns provided further incentive for the Tribes to diversify. Some of the Tribes' smaller enterprises, caught between their dual mandates of providing services and employment for the reservation and turning a profit, felt a greater pressure to operate in the black; and some programs that started simply as services, such as tribal credit and the housing department, became profit-making ventures. Just before the recession hit, tribal members stopped saying "no" long enough to vote for the hydroelectric project, bringing some needed income diversity. But it was a slow growth period and a time for self-examination.

If the whole purpose of this corporate adventure had been to create jobs and improve the quality of life on the reservation, why were so many people still idle* and unhappy? Why did people still feel powerless to direct their lives? As the tribal corporation had blossomed, it had seemed to take on a life of its own; people had to keep reminding their leaders that the corporation was there to serve them and not to perpetuate itself. Yet in providing for tribal members, the huge administrative and service structure had to be careful not to smother people in the paternalistic manner of the BIA. As the tribal organization had grown in confidence and sophistication, a gap had developed and widened between the people and their leaders. The people were proud of their successful business and the tribal members helping to direct it, but they were apt to feel resentment, too, toward a structure that was becoming as overwhelming as the one hundred year presence of the federal government.

One symbol of this domination was the ever-present white employee. So intent had the Tribes been on succeeding financially, that they sought talent outside the reservation population to fill key jobs. This was always done with the understanding that tribal members would be trained to take over one day. But many of the non-Indians, tempted by generous tribal salaries and benefits or genuinely stimulated by the challenge of the work itself, stayed on. Tribal members who went off to college or special training often returned to find nothing but entry level jobs, and opted for better paid, unskilled jobs at the mill or in the woods, or for off-reservation careers. They bitterly accused white employees of empire-building, bringing in their friends and families, and, if they ever left, driving away in big new cars and carrying good-looking resumes.

Those tribal members who did work their way up

---

*Unemployment on the reservation averages around thirty percent, a figure that is somewhat misleading in that it includes all those available for work, not just those actively seeking work.

146

through the tribal organization felt justifiably protective when the budget-cutting of the late 1970s and early 1980s began. By that time, the Tribes had begun to piece together health and social services programs to address some of the community's lingering problems. When the budget axe was poised over jobs and social programs, there was an outcry. It had taken a long time for the "soft side" of the tribal organization to develop and the people did not want to lose what they had gained.

The scope of reservation development was scaled down to more modest projects. For example, the twice-rejected four million dollar detention center and justice facility evolved into an expansion and renovation of the existing jail. Meanwhile, an in-depth examination of the tribal law enforcement system was aimed at improving the substance, and not just the packaging, of justice programs. Around the same time, the whole tribal structure was reorganized to separate administrative and fiscal functions from community services, decentralize management, and increase efficiency and accountability. The education department refocused on grooming tribal members for successful employment. Tribal health programs were given a long, hard look and the problem of alcohol and drug abuse was assigned top priority.

It was a period of constructive engagement between the Tribes and the people, probably best reflected in the launching of the reservation's second comprehensive development plan in 1981. This time, Tribal Council and planners decided to go straight to the people with surveys and open meetings to ascertain their ideas and concerns in five main areas: human resources, natural resources, recreation, housing, and forest lands. The resulting data is expected to be as helpful in reservation planning for the next twenty years as the OSU study has been in the last twenty.

Tribal members seemed appeased for a time, but their concerns boiled up in 1985 when, for the first time since the tribal government and corporation were established in 1938, the annual tribal budget was petitioned and rejected by voters in a tribal referendum.

The reservation was without operating monies for 1986, beyond the Council's twenty-five thousand dollar line-item authority. Tribal member employees nervously considered the possibility of losing their jobs while quietly applauding the petitioners.

At community meetings during the fall of 1985 and well into 1986, petitioners and other members expressed their distrust of non-Indian managers, their desire for more information about how the Tribal Council makes its decisions, and their feeling that it was high time Indians were running their own reservation. Tribal Council, unable to elicit any specific suggestions for budget changes, pledged to be more accountable to its constituents, raised the monthly per capita, and posted a second, nearly identical budget, which was not petitioned. A regularly scheduled election that spring produced an almost entirely new Council, including one of the petitioners, but it would take some time to mend the rifts that had opened up not just between members and leaders, but between and within families.

Another frustration of some tribal members through the "boomtown" years was the Tribes' tendency to favor tribal over individual enterprise. The BIA may have failed in the last century to create Indian entrepreneurs from a communal people, but in the 1980s the tables are turning. Now many tribal members, in a kind of natural drift toward the more competitive values of the surrounding culture, are clamoring for more individual business opportunities and fewer tribally owned and operated enterprises.

A number of tribal members have taken advantage of low interest tribal credit, one dollar a year tribal land leases, or tribal expertise to become successful entrepreneurs, but others feel their dreams have been discouraged by the huge tribal service umbrella. There are loggers, truckers, commercial fishermen, ranchers, Christmas tree cutters, restaurant owners, a gravel pit operator, a service station operator, a hairdresser—but they compose only a small percentage of the work force. Countless others make partial incomes from beadwork, sewing, jewelry-making, babysitting,

A cast aluminum sculpture of a rootdigger by Richard Byer of Seattle stands outside the tribal administration building, a reminder to tribal and BIA employees that traditional culture lives on at Warm Springs. (Cynthia D. Stowell)

ranching, or home franchises; but most working adults are on the tribal payroll. Tribal planning has favored business that will benefit the whole population, but people are now saying that they would be better served by an atmosphere of enterprise and initiative.

This concern would no doubt be viewed as a luxury by the nation's less prosperous tribes, many of which are still on the dreaming end of successful tribal enterprises. Warm Springs is decades ahead of most other tribes in developing its resources and securing a consistent income, a position it reached with minimal encouragement from the federal government. Aside from extending certain tax advantages and making EDA loans and grants available to tribes, the govern-

ment was for a long time blind to the economic potential of the tribal corporations it helped create in the 1930s. A report filed in 1984 by the President's Commission on Indian Reservation Economies finally acknowledged impediments to reservation development and suggested ways that tribes might be freed up to compete more aggressively in the business world. Some Indian leaders see the report as evidence that the government wants to step aside before tribes are ready to stand on their own, but others feel it is the beginning of new opportunities. As other tribes feel their way through the maze of economic development, Warm Springs' place as a role model may become increasingly important, and the questions it is asking now about tribal versus individual enterprise and corporate versus cultural gains may soon be universal reservation concerns.

For the Warm Springs people, it has been a long, interesting, and sometimes awkward transition from hunting and gathering to competing in the twentieth century marketplace. A visit to the tribal administration building, where several hundred glassed-in employees pore over computer printouts, electronically transmit memos to Washington, D.C., or confer with high-priced consultants, makes it look easy and complete. But the Tribes are constantly having to come to terms with where they have been and where they want to go.

Warm Springs is not a "failed experiment in socialism," as Secretary of the Interior James Watt called Indian reservations of the 1980s. On the contrary, it has a good start on achieving an enviable balance of corporate strength, communal benefit, and individual initiative. ☐

A COMPROMISED SOVEREIGNTY

VISITORS TO THE Warm Springs Reservation often feel they have entered a foreign country. In a sense they have. The people look and sound different, and they embrace cultural traditions and values that set them apart from other Americans. Less visibly, the reservation also has a political identity distinct from the counties, state, and nation that surround it. In its quasi-sovereignty, the reservation is at once a land apart and a web of intersecting laws, jurisdictions, and citizenships—a source of confusion for seasoned attorneys and vacationers alike. ☐ One of the most difficult things for first-time visitors to understand is that they are on private land with the tacit permission of its owner, the Confederated Tribes. While held in trust by the federal government, it is not public land, and tribal law prevails. This does not explain, however, why a speeding ticket written by a state trooper on U.S. Highway 26 is paid to Jefferson or Wasco County, why a fly fisherman needs both state and tribal licenses, why logging roads are regulated by the Department of Interior, or why it is against federal law to sell beer at Macy's Store. The explanation lies in a long, piecemeal history of legislation, court decisions, and negotiated agreements that have attempted to define the status of the Warm Springs and other Indian people. The unique blend of dependence and sovereignty that exists on Indian reservations has been hundreds of years in the making, but it is still a fragile and much misunderstood arrangement. ☐ When Europeans first encountered the native peoples of North America, their autonomy was not an issue. It was easy to view the strange and exotic cultures as wholly separate and ungovernable. Early settlers, explorers, and trappers valued the Indians'

150

knowledge of the land and how to survive on it, and missionaries set about introducing them to Christianity and other "civilizing" influences. But as settlements grew, commerce quickened, and colonial governments took shape, there developed a need to formalize relations with the tribes and define ways in which the two peoples would inhabit the continent.

The British monarchy's Proclamation of 1763 drew the first of many lines around the colonies, beyond which the Indians were to live undisturbed; it also took away from the colonies the privilege of regulating trade with the Indians. After the American Revolution, during which the Indians tended to side with the less threatening British, the Continental Congress re-affirmed both the idea of a separate "Indian country" and the centralization of authority over Indian affairs. But by placing this authority in the new War Department, the government was also acknowledging its chosen way of dealing with them. (Indian Affairs became part of the Department of Interior in 1849.) The longstanding "Indian problem", which the Indians certainly viewed as a white problem, was growing as the new nation pushed on its western borders. Very simply, the Indians were in the way.

Generations of Americans would experiment with solutions, ranging from "assimilation" and "civilization" to "removal" (a term meaning anything from relocation to extermination). Essentially, the government spent its first century at war with the natives, sanctioning frontier hostilities and glamourizing Indian fighters and the frontier's "Indian Wars." With the military as a tool of persuasion, the government began pressing treaties on the tribes, who by the mid-nineteenth century were worn down by decades of strife and dissension among their own members over how to deal with the white presence. The treaty-making period, which officially lasted until 1871, had started in the colonial days with treaties of commerce, but in the nineteenth century the main intent of treaties was to make peace and acquire land. The principal way of achieving both was to move the tribes to reservations.

Once tribes were subdued and confined on government-held land, their status as separate nations no longer seemed obvious or important. Many of the treaties, including the one with the Columbia River tribes, contained language that hinted at the new relationship with the federal government. Article 7 of the Treaty of 1855 states:

> The confederated bands acknowledge their dependence on the Government of the United States . . . (and) further engage to submit to and observe all laws, rules, and regulations which may be prescribed by the United States for the government of said Indians.

This notion of dependence on the federal government was consistent with the language of a definitive court judgment made in Georgia more than twenty years before. In a series of cases involving the Cherokee Nation, Chief Justice John Marshall attempted to sort out the rights of state government and the United States with regard to Indian tribes, and in so doing, laid down the guiding principles that have since shaped U.S. Indian policy. In *The Cherokee Nation* v. *The State of Georgia* (1831), Justice Marshall coined the enigmatic but enduring term "domestic dependent nations" to describe the status of Indian tribes vis-à-vis the federal government. Although the decision did not answer directly the question of Georgia's right to intervene in the Cherokees' effort to establish their own constitution and government, Marshall did set forth a framework for future dealings with tribes. He wrote:

> Though the Indians are acknowledged to have an unquestionable and, heretofore, unquestioned right to the lands they occupy . . . yet it may well be doubted whether those tribes which reside within the acknowledged boundaries of the United States can, with strict accuracy, be denominated foreign nations. They may, more correctly, perhaps, be denominated domestic dependent nations. . . . Their relation to the United States resembles that of a ward to its guardian.
>
> They look to our government for protection; rely upon its kindness and power; appeal to it for relief to their wants; and address the president as their great father.

151

The next year, in *Worcester* v. *Georgia* (1832), Justice Marshall confirmed the federal government's exclusive right to make laws affecting the Cherokees and their territory. This decision, which limited the state's powers, also contained language that Indian tribes today cite in their assertion of tribal sovereignty. It describes the "several Indian nations" as being "distinct political communities, having territorial boundaries, within which their authority is exclusive."

Just as these closely related court decisions describe the simultaneous dependence and autonomy of Indian tribes, so too did the treaties mark both an end and a beginning for tribes in their struggle to preserve their sovereignty. The treaties that so sharply limited the power and liberty of their Indian signers, provide today—as the "supreme law of the land"—the basis for the tribes' ability to govern themselves and enjoy certain privileges. Treaties define a special relationship between Indian tribes and the U.S. Government, but, for all its protective nature, it is a relationship that can be terminated unilaterally by the government. The sovereignty of Indian tribes is compromised by the fact that a single Congressional act can dissolve a reservation or a tribe and its whole legal and political identity. While a terminated tribe could conceivably become a corporation, city, or county, its existence as a tribal government is dependent on the will of the federal government.

FROM AUTONOMY TO DEPENDENCE

It may have been easy for the white newcomers to the continent to realize they were dealing with separate nations, but it was more difficult for them to respect the manner in which the native peoples governed themselves. Except for the Iroquois Confederacy of New York and the so-called Five Civilized Tribes of the Southeast, whose governments resembled, and in fact inspired, the democratic federalism of the new American nation, most tribes' traditional methods for keeping order and making decisions were either misunderstood or dismissed as primitive by Anglo onlookers. It was difficult for the white man with his European political traditions to understand the infor-

mal, sometimes even mystical, decision-making process of the Indian tribes.

In the case of the Columbia River and Great Basin people, traditional governing was largely a matter of arriving at a consensus, utilizing the expert and respected advice of certain headmen. Headmen might remind their people of the values and standards by which members of the community were expected to live, but enforcement came more from peer pressure and the punitive functions of shamans. Special tasks, such as warfare or, among the Paiutes, rabbit or antelope drives, were usually carried out by individuals other than the headmen.

Among the Wascos and Sahaptins, political organization did not go beyond the village level; the villages did not have a collective political identity. Decision-making among the Paiutes occurred at the level of the extended family. There is some indication that with pressure from white settlers and with the influence of Plains culture, the people of the Plateau began to develop tribal identities and the function of the war "chiefs" became more distinct.* These new dynamics seem to have affected the interior Sahaptins and Wascos less than those groups on the eastern edge of the Plateau, however. In the Great Basin, there was a more obvious trend in the mid-nineteenth century toward grouping together in mounted, highly mobile bands under charismatic leaders such as Panaina, Wewa and Oits of the Northern Paiutes.

Village autonomy and group consensus tended to be cumbersome in the face of rapid-paced treaty making, and it was often simply overlooked by white "negotiators" for the sake of convenience. Oregon Territory's Superintendent for Indian Affairs, Joel Palmer, had been among the river people long enough to know and understand their political processes, and while he clearly acknowledged village or "band" leadership during the negotiating and signing of the 1855 treaty, his grouping of Sahaptins and Wascos together into one

---

* Verne F. Ray, *Cultural Relations in the Plateau of Northwestern America*, and Christopher Miller, *Prophetic Worlds*. Miller would disagree on the matter of Plains influence.

152

treaty was a geographic expedience that sidestepped political and ethnographic distinctions.

Traditional government all but died when the treaty was signed. The language of the treaty arbitrarily restructured their leadership by arranging for the election of one head chief for the newly confederated "bands" and a chief for each of what were considered the "three principal bands": the Upper and Lower Deschutes bands of Sahaptins, and the "Wascopum" band of the Wascos. The treaty attempted to ensconce these chiefs by awarding them each a house and ten acres of fenced and plowed land, as well as a guaranteed twenty-year salary for the head chief. Today, three chiefs represent the Warm Springs, Wasco, and Paiute tribes. The manner in which they receive their bonnets varies widely, from inheritance or appointment by an elder to election by secret ballot. And once selected, the chiefs have an unclear but largely ceremonial mandate outside their participation on Tribal Council.

This disruption of the traditional political organization of the river people was profound and permanent. Beyond the procedural changes in leadership imposed by the treaty lay the fact that there was virtually nothing left for the people to decide for themselves. The power of the government in the form of the BIA was absolute. Even chiefly guidance on when to fish or gather roots, how to handle disputes, or what to teach the children, was dependent on the will of the government's officials. What is more, the people were being governed by, and were expected to be obedient to, a nation that did not extend citizenship to them until 1924.

Long before the people of Warm Springs had any real sense of the magnitude and nature of the United States, their allegiance was being groomed. The children in the BIA boarding school arose early every morning to raise the American flag and sing patriotic songs like "America" and "Hooray for the Fourth of July." Adult men were conscripted as scouts for the U.S. Army in campaigns against the "Snake" (Paiute) Indians in 1866 and the Modocs in 1873, although the treaty forbade the tribes from making their own war except in self-defense. Since then, through the world wars and Asian conflicts, military voluntarism has been a source of great pride on the reservation. Stripped of the powers associated with nationhood, the tribes at Warm Springs transferred at least some of their allegiance to the "great father."

Today, the reservation's Fourth of July and Veterans Day celebrations attract participation from towns all over central Oregon, and the colors are posted faithfully at state occasions and powwows alike. The flag motif also shows up frequently in their beadwork. But their patriotism exists alongside a slow-burning resentment for the many years of stagnation and impotence caused by their lost autonomy.

A NEW KIND OF AUTONOMY

Tribes all over the United States were given the opportunity to regain a measure of control over their own people and futures with the Indian Reorganization (Wheeler-Howard) Act of 1934. This particular swing of the federal policy pendulum acknowledged the failure of the government's usurpation of reservation decision-making and provided a new structure for self-government based on both Anglo and tribal traditions. The Wheeler-Howard Act has been criticized by some as a further attempt on the part of the government to acculturate Indians, this time by mass-producing constitutions and pressing tribes to approve them. But at the very least, it promised an interruption in the pattern of unilateral policy-making that had one generation of white legislators correcting the mistakes of the previous generation while creating more problems for the next. Nothing had worked; the Indians continued to resist assimilation while becoming increasingly dependent on the government. The fresh eyes and thorough research of social reformer John Collier saw a way out of the cycle, and when he became commissioner of Indian Affairs he helped push through the reforming legislation.

In Warm Springs, legal help was sought and the Wheeler-Howard constitution was tailored to meet local needs. The hope and strength embodied in this document are clear in its preamble, which echoes the U.S. Constitution:

We, the Confederated Tribes of the Warm Springs Reservation of Oregon, in order to establish a more responsible and effective organization to promote our general welfare, conserve and develop our lands and other resources, and secure to ourselves and our posterity the power to exercise certain rights of self-government not inconsistent with existing federal and state laws, do ordain and establish this Constitution.

Tribal members approved the constitution in December 1937 by a 181–77 vote, and it was approved by the Department of Interior the following February.

The Warm Springs constitution provides for a Tribal Council composed of eleven members. Eight are elected for three-year terms to represent three voting districts that roughly correspond to the Warm Springs, Wasco, and Paiute tribes: Simnasho is represented by three members, Agency by three, and Seekseequa by two. The other three Council members are the tribal chiefs, who serve for life. This system, called "apportionment," was challenged in 1986 by tribal members who felt that the reservation as a whole would be better served if all eleven Council representatives were elected at large, eliminating districts and the automatic participation of chiefs. A referendum in 1986 left the system as it had been since 1937.

The Tribal Council was empowered by the constitution to govern the Warm Springs people with ordinances of its own making and to manage the economic affairs of the reservation. Council's twenty-one specific powers boil down to these functions: appropriating tribal funds for public use; overseeing the use of tribal land and resources; protecting the health, security, and welfare of tribal members; advising and consulting with the Department of Interior on all matters affecting the reservation; and negotiating with the federal, state, and local governments on behalf of the Confederated Tribes. These executive, legislative, and corporate powers, as broad and complete as they are, must have seemed a heady turn of events for the Warm Springs people. But they were ready. With self-rule returned to them after nearly a century, the

people elected the best of their peers to take them into this new era.

The Wheeler-Howard Act created a new image of the Indian leader. The paid, paper-swamped councilman elected by secret ballot, meeting at regularly appointed times according to Robert's Rules of Order seemed very different from the traditional headman who was simply on hand when his people needed him. Council members today meet two or three times a week, and sometimes more, for daylong sessions, during which they might address such diverse agenda items as approving a position statement on a proposed national policy, granting money to a bereaved family member for funeral expenses, discussing bank erosion in reservation creeks, or reviewing The Tribe's annual operating budget. Their oak meeting table is piled high with papers that cannot possibly be read in full by the part-time representatives, but they have exercised well their constitutional right to employ legal counsel to advise them on particularly complex issues or to handle some of the tedious paperwork. Yet it is ultimately that same brand of wisdom and instinct their forebears possessed which has enabled the Council to steer through crises and plan its future with a farsightedness that other governments would surely envy.

Tribal government at Warm Springs is overseen by the "general council," comprised of the voting members of the Tribes, who are defined by the constitution as all those tribal members over twenty-one or married. Certain issues such as major expenditures outside the annual budget and adoption of new members are put to the vote of the general council. A slightly different body of voters, those tribal members over eighteen and registered with the BIA, participates in infrequent "secretarial" elections called by the Secretary of the Interior for changes in the constitution and by-laws or the corporate charter.

Members of the general council may present issues to or challenge the decisions of the Tribal Council through a petition and referendum process, exercised twice recently when the 1986 budget was rejected and apportionment was challenged. They may also partici-

The first Tribal Council at Warm Springs was formed in 1938. Members were: (front row) Sam Wewa, (Supt. Elliott, not a member), Fred Wagner, Oliver Kalama; (second row) Frank Queahpama, Sr., James Johnson, George Meachem (secretary/treasurer), Moses Hellon, William McCorkle; (standing) Frank Winishut, Isaac McKinley, Joe McCorkle. (Courtesy of the Confederated Tribes)

pate in their government by seeking appointments to any of a dozen committees that advise Tribal Council on matters ranging from fish and wildlife management to health and welfare.

The intent of the Indian Reorganization Act was to place decision-making back in the hands of the tribes, which naturally meant a reduction in the role of the BIA on reservations. It did not change the substance of the tribes' relationship with the government; the U.S. was still trustee of reservation lands and resources and was still bound by the treaties it had signed. But the tone and the dynamics of that relationship changed to varying degrees depending on the readiness of the tribes to take over.

At Warm Springs, the weaning process was steady and sure. The Department of the Interior, in the person of the reservation agent or superintendent, for many years formed the backbone of administrative and technical services on the reservation. But as the tribal organization and its expertise grew, the balance of power gradually tilted. Today, the superintendent's presence on the reservation is low key, at times almost titular. He is not unlike an ambassador from the U.S., on hand to help the Tribes interpret and carry out their trust relationship with the federal government. The superintendent still signs all Council resolutions and ordinances and he administers those BIA programs that remain on the reservation for technical and advisory reasons, such as forestry, range conservation, some law enforcement, fire protection, realty services, facilities management, and some human resource programs. Most other services are provided by the Tribes, either with their own funds or under contract with the Bureau. It was certainly a sign of the times when the Tribes built their own administration building in 1977 and the BIA found itself in the rather unaccustomed position of leasing space from them. It is important to remember, however, that Warm Springs is unusual among Indian reservations, most of which are so lacking in resources and opportunities that they must continue to depend heavily on the federal agency for services, employment, and direction.

Some tribal members at Warm Springs worry that their government is starting to resemble the sprawling, paternalistic bureaucracy that it replaced fifty years ago. They are only dimly aware of the activities of their elected representatives, who, they feel, are making decisions behind closed doors for the benefit of the people but without the participation of the people. It is the same periodic alienation that occurs between any representative government and its constituents, except that the expectations may be greater for a people with a recent tradition of consensus. When tribal members complain, Warm Springs leaders are apt to remind them that their constitutional government has given reservation politics a stability that other tribes without constitutions (e.g. their relatives, the Yakimas) have not enjoyed.

STILL IN THE INDIAN BUSINESS

The success of Warm Springs in running its own affairs was symbolized by the 1980 appointment of the Tribes' general manager to the position of assistant secretary of the Interior for Indian Affairs in Washington, D.C. During his four years in the capital, Ken Smith, who had been Vernon Jackson's protege and successor, helped the Reagan Administration formulate an Indian policy that reaffirmed the government's trust relationship with Indian tribes while promising to "remove impediments" to developing tribal self-government and reservation economies. Smith also had to make difficult cuts in the BIA budget, aiming at administrative waste while trying to preserve the integrity of reservation programs. But the Reagan/Smith policies, along with simultaneous cutbacks in other federal assistance, have made tribal leaders suspicious. Their spoken fear is that the federal government is slowly getting out of the "Indian business."

Anxiety about the government severing its ties with Indian tribes is not unfounded when viewed in light of recent history. After years of assimilation efforts, the government in the 1950s apparently thought it had been so successful that it was time to give the prosperous tribes their "freedom." The resultant termination policy was an ill-conceived and unilateral method of ending the trust relationship by literally buying out the reservations, turning the money over to

the individual tribal members, and withdrawing all federal support and protection. Members of terminated tribes were no longer recognized as Indians by the government, treaties were nothing but yellowed pieces of paper, and tribal land bases were gone. Termination was supposedly implemented with permission of affected tribes, but elections were usually hurried and often widely misunderstood. Indian voters, unsophisticated in their knowledge of Indian law and the trust relationship, saw the sums of money involved and opted for termination.

In Oregon, three reservations—Klamath, Siletz, and Grand Ronde—and a total of sixty-one tribal groups were terminated. The Klamaths most resembled Warm Springs in that they had valuable timberland among their 862,000 acres of land in south-central Oregon, which they had been exploiting successfully since early in the century. The tribe's land base and economic future were converted into short-lived individual wealth when private companies bought up some of the acreage and the rest became Winema National Forest. But the Klamath Tribe, although no longer recognized by the federal government, maintained a kind of loose, working identity that allowed them to fight successfully for fishing and hunting rights in their aboriginal territory and then for reinstatement as a federally recognized tribe (in 1986). The Siletz Tribe, whose members had scattered to urban areas after termination in 1957, united to wage a long struggle for restoration in the 1970s, winning back their federal status in 1977 and a small land base not long after. Several other coastal tribes have also been restored, but without the return of land.

It may seem ironic that tribes forced onto reservations in the nineteenth century were, in the twentieth century, asking to have their terminated reservations back. What they had bargained for at the treaty tables when they had given up much of their aboriginal claims was a protected land base on which they could operate outside the constraints of local residents and their governments. Termination pulled the rug out from under some of the most successful tribes by not only eliminating the land, which was the foundation for their economic development, but also by eliminat-

ing the autonomy that had exempted them from local taxation and regulation.

Though the Confederated Tribes of Warm Springs were not directly affected by the termination policy, they saw in their neighbor Oregon tribes, and other successful tribes around the country, a disaster that could just as well have been visited on them. If there is one word that consistently strikes fear into the hearts of Indians nationwide, it is "termination." When President Nixon signed the Indian Self-Determination and Educational Assistance Act (P.L. 93-638) in 1975, tacitly ending the termination era, tribes suspected it was "termination in disguise," a long-term preparation for eventual abandonment.

But in many ways, the Self-Determination Act reflected a progressive new trend in government policy, a logical continuation of the reforms of the 1930s. The legislation itself encouraged tribal control of reservation programs by making it easier for tribes to contract with the government to provide their own reservation services. Perhaps more important than the actual 93-638 contracting procedures, which were initially cumbersome and slow to implement, were the implications of a new self-determination for Indian tribes. By fostering the development of stronger tribal administration while reaffirming its own continuing trust responsibility, the government was essentially getting out of the way of the tribes.

The era of self-determination has been a time of sweeping legislative and judicial successes and gathering strength among Indian tribes. It was born in the social foment of the 1960s when Indian voices joined the chorus of demands for human rights around the country and "Red Power" became a slogan for young Indians with raised fists. Wounded Knee, Alcatraz, and the takeover of the BIA headquarters in Washington, D.C. were very visible signs of the struggle of Indians against their "great father." The "red brothers and sisters" of AIM, the American Indian Movement, forced America to look at the injustices that had led to high infant mortality, alcoholism, suicide, and poverty among Indian populations.

While Warm Springs has always looked askance at radical politics, it unquestionably reaped benefits when

157

In a tradition of cooperation and friendly relations with Oregon's governors, tribal representatives met with Governor Tom McCall in 1967 to inform him of their purchase of the sawmill at Warm Springs and the start-up on their tribal wood-products enterprise. In the delegation were (from left) General Manager of the Tribes Vernon Jackson, Councilman Olney Patt, Sr., public relations consultant William Marsh, Councilman Charlie Jackson, owner of the purchased mill Samuel Johnson, and tribal attorney Owen Panner. (Courtesy of the Confederated Tribes)

the government and the courts began to respond with reforms in the 1970s. Once the public's shoulders had been sufficiently shaken, it was the particular talent of the Warm Springs leaders to smooth over any rough spots with a canny but gentle negotiating stance.

The late 1960s and 1970s were a golden time for Indian tribes, when many important gains were made. Their land base grew for the first time in centuries as claims were settled in their favor; BIA budget allocations increased; tribes were winning major federal court cases upholding their treaty rights to resources on and off reservations; and several key pieces of legislation were passed, including P.L. 93–638, the Indian Education Act, a Senate Joint Resolution to protect Indian religious freedom, the Indian Health Care Improvement Act, the Indian Child Welfare Act, restoration acts, and to the north, the Alaska Native Claims Settlement Act. The Bureau of Indian Affairs became more of an advocate than an authority by instituting Indian preference in hiring and launching programs such as "Buy Indian;" and other segments of the government, particularly the departments of Com-

Congressman Al Ullman was a valued friend of the Confederated Tribes, as evidenced by the gift headdress presented to him in his Washington, D.C. offices by Wasco Chief Nelson Wallulatum in 1975. As Oregon's Senior Representative and Chairman of the Ways and Means Committee, Ullman actively supported the Tribe's development efforts, from sponsorship of the McQuinn Strip legislation to assistance in buying back the Kah-Nee-Ta site. (George Ortez / N.E.W.S. Photo N.W.)

merce and of Health, Education, and Welfare, became more responsive to the social and economic needs of reservations.

Across the country, a sense of unity was developing among the diverse and isolated tribes. For decades the government had ignored tribal differences for the sake of policy-making; while this tendency was very destructive to Indian culture, it eventually produced a common ground for tribes nationwide and a focus for their reform activities. Indian leaders had been traveling to Washington, D.C. in ceremonial delegations for

more than a century, but in the last twenty years, tribes have become sophisticated and powerful lobbyists, well-versed in legislative procedure, alert to impending bills and court cases, and ready to share information with each other through national tribal organizations and the growing Indian media.

This sophistication, along with a winning streak in Congress and courts, inevitably brought on a conservative "backlash" from America's mainstream, but it also ensured that the tribes would survive such counter-attacks. Western congressmen, whose constituents

were ranchers, farmers, mineral developers, and fishermen, began to introduce bills in the late 1970s to reduce the tribes' control over their own land, to limit fishing and water rights, and even to abrogate treaties. But vigilant Indian leaders and their congressional allies saw to it that such bills never made it through committees, and the federal government has continued to affirm its trust responsibility and to honor its treaties with Indian tribes.

Despite all the gains made in the 1970s, tribes are still wary when it comes to their relationship to the federal government. With some regularity, a bureaucrat or legislator suggests weaving a particular Indian program into the general fabric of the government, such as recent attempts to move BIA education programs into the Department of Education and change Indian Health Services to an entitlement program like other Public Health Service programs. Of course, this ignores the fact that the programs exist especially for Indians not because they are of a certain ethnic or economic group, but because they are governments that made treaties with the U.S. government. In 1985, tribes objected strenuously when a presidential commission on reservation economies recommended that the "Byzantine" BIA be dismantled and that a trimmer Indian Trust Services Administration take its place. Indians have long criticized the BIA for being overgrown, full of waste, and uninterested in real progress on reservations, but it is also a symbol of the government's continuing trust responsibility. After 160 years, tribes like Warm Springs are learning how to work best with the BIA to promote tribal self-sufficiency and discourage dependence. To switch agencies midstream might be to lose that momentum.

Again in 1987, tribes were faced with a series of unilateral proposals from the Department of Interior that seemed to undermine the government's trust responsibility. Warm Springs took a leading role in resisting such initiatives as the transfer of Indian trust funds to a private bank and the "privatization" of reservation forest management, move that tribal leaders regard as a dismantling of the BIA.

Treaties and Supreme Court decisions may be "the supreme law of the land," but the special relationship they created between Indian tribes and the federal government is still surprisingly tenuous. The very existence of a reservation and its government has been, and could again be, eliminated by a vote of Congress and the stroke of a President's pen. All it would take is for Indians to be either too much of a "problem" or too successful, and political expediency would prevail. Tribes, then, are forced to walk a thin line between dependence and self-reliance, failure and success, in order to survive.

GOVERNMENT TO GOVERNMENT

If it has been difficult for the federal government to grapple with its relationship with Indian tribes, the nature of tribal governments has been even more of a mystery to local governments. The Confederated Tribes of Warm Springs have excelled in their diplomacy and cooperation with other governments, but even so, misconceptions abound.

The fact that the people of the Columbia River and the high desert lived in what is now Oregon for thousands of years before newcomers established a territory, a state, and local governments, is only part of the reason that Warm Springs enjoys relative independence from state and local governments. More important is the fact that the federal government and the courts have repeatedly affirmed the status of Indian tribes as separate governments. "They were here first" is a legitimate ethical argument; that they continue to be sovereign governments is the more useful legal argument. As an Oregon expert in Indian law so aptly expressed it, "Indian tribes are governments, not Elks Clubs."* This is difficult for other governments to understand; Indians are more popularly viewed as a minority or subculture, not a political entity.

With the state of Oregon, Warm Springs enjoys an amiable, if aloof, relationship. Governor Victor Atiyeh came into office in 1978 with a good record on Indian issues, having supported and served on the State

---

*Thanks to Charles Wilkinson for this remark, made at a tribal sovereignty workshop in 1984.

Commission on Indian Services (established in 1975 as the only legislative commission advising a state on Indian affairs). Atiyeh's popularity with Warm Springs continued into his second term and he was a familiar face on the reservation, where, in cowboy hat and boots, he has been a parade marshal, keynote speaker, and an annual guest at the Pi-Ume-Sha powwow. Tribal leaders have been similarly welcome in the governor's office in Salem, not as colorful visitors but as representatives of viable governments.

Previous governors, as well as state and federal legislators, have also had warm relations with Warm Springs, a situation that tribes in other western states find almost unbelievable. While there is some feeling in Oregon from time to time that if Indians can vote and benefit from state services, they should also be taxed and subject to all state laws and regulations, the issue has not generated the emotional fervor it has in other states.

Relations with Oregon might be more strained and certainly more complex if Warm Springs had been included in a 1953 federal law (P.L. 280) that gave certain Western states civil and criminal jurisdiction on Indian reservations. Through much hard work and persuasion, Warm Springs leaders succeeded in exempting their reservation from P.L. 280, thus preserving its autonomy and the integrity of its law enforcement and judicial system. In fact, it was the stability of this system that worked in the Tribes' favor while they resisted P.L. 280.

For all the criticism the tribal justice system receives from the community it serves, and for all the challenges that tribal courts universally field from more "sophisticated" legal quarters, Warm Springs has a solid, working system well able to enforce the law-and-order code created by Tribal Council. Three lay judges, all Indian, hear cases involving civil violations and misdemeanors, but the fourteen major felonies are remanded to federal court. The Tribal Court also has limited civil jurisdiction over non-Indians, although defendants can request a change of venue.

The Tribal Court, which operates with Tribal Council oversight but outside of the tribal organization, is assisted by prosecutors, defenders, and parole/proba-

tion officers, all hired by the Tribes. Backing up the court is the tribal police department, a cadre of Indian and non-Indian officers empowered to enforce tribal law and cross-deputized with the sheriff's departments in Wasco and Jefferson counties. At one time, all law enforcement was provided by the BIA, but now the only remaining BIA staff are two investigators and a secretary.

The tendency of the Tribal justice system in recent years has been to incorporate non-Indian legal procedures and move farther away from traditional forms. The Indian Civil Rights Act of 1968, which extended the civil rights that citizens enjoy under the U.S. Constitution to Indians vis-à-vis their tribal governments, did much to Anglicize tribal courts. Though the Warm Springs constitution already contained a bill of rights providing for speedy and public hearings, due notice, and trial by jury, the threat of review by higher, off-reservation courts has put pressure on the Tribes to be as thorough as possible in procedural details. The more the tribal court resembles non-Indian courts, of course, the more credibility it has with other jurisdictions, too. But it loses credibility with tribal members, as when fines and jail terms were suddenly imposed on people failing to appear for jury duty, the result of a recent revision of the tribal law and order code that brought it more in line with the state code. There are some who wonder what value tribal sovereignty has if the tribes are simply going to imitate Anglo systems.

The Tribes' ability to handle its own judicial affairs has been a factor in discouraging damaging legislation (P.L. 280) and hastening positive legislation such as the Indian Child Welfare Act (1978), which gives jurisdiction to tribal courts in foster and adoptive placement of Indian children on or off reservations. Tribes nationwide, including Warm Springs, wrote and lobbied for this legislation in an effort to regain control over the future of children whom state courts often placed with non-Indian families, effectively severing cultural ties. Passage of this bill was a good example of tribes using their legal expertise and governmental powers to achieve cultural ends.

The Warm Springs Reservation is said to lie in Jefferson and Wasco counties, although whether the

county lines actually extend through the reservation is a matter of some debate. One former tribal police chief, while vigorously promoting the cross-deputization of tribal and county policy officers, just as vigorously maintained that the reservation is not within either county but is wholly separate and autonomous. In fact, the relationship between the Tribes and the counties is similar to the tribal-state relationship. For the purposes of elections and school district representation, and for some social services, the people on the reservation are considered residents of one or the other county. But neither county can tax reservation land, a sore point with local citizens who feel that the Indians have representation without taxation.

There are, however, two official and many unofficial ways in which the counties receive revenue from the Tribes. When the Round Butte and Pelton Dam agreements were negotiated with Portland General Electric in the 1950s, the Tribes insisted that the projects be kept on the tax rolls to ensure continued funding of county and school district budgets. Another source of school district funding comes from the federal government in lieu of taxes to help pay for the education of children living on federal land (also included under P.L. 874 are military bases). Warm Springs children, who comprise roughly thirty to forty percent of the student population in Jefferson County School District 509-J, also bring in federal funds earmarked for Indian enrichment programs. But many people feel the reservation still does not pull its weight financially.

In 1979, when tribal leaders and the school board's one Indian member requested that Warm Springs Elementary be included in a district-wide building renovation program, the school board launched an examination of the Tribes' financial impact on the area served by the 509-J school district. The report showed that through dam revenues and federal monies, tribal payroll, and consumerism, the Tribes contributed more than its share to the county and its educational programs. The renovations were never approved, but a point had been made.

Despite setbacks, Warm Springs has made steady progress in its assertion that it is a government parallel with state, county, and municipal governments. The talent of Warm Springs leaders in personal diplomacy has been a powerful asset, even at the national level. The passage of the 1983 Tribal Tax Status Act, for which Warm Springs leaders and attorneys argued long and convincingly, was one recent victory. That act recognizes the right of Indian tribes to levy taxes, float bonds, and otherwise raise revenues as local governments do.

It has always been a struggle for Warm Springs and tribal groups across the nation to prove their inherent sovereignty, even though it has been upheld in treaties and courts since early in the nineteenth century. But the more experience that Indian tribes have in exercising their governmental powers, the harder it will be for non-Indians to simply dismiss them as just so many Elks Clubs. ☐

162

CULTURAL JOURNEY

AMID THE SOUND of rushing water and a crackling fire, a hushed voice on the radio enticed: "Kah-Nee-Ta. Not just another resort. Another culture." Guests of Kah-Nee-Ta found they could partake of barbecued salmon, sleep in a tepee, watch powwow dancing, and purchase locally made crafts. This romantic and controlled glimpse of the Warm Springs Reservation may have satisfied some people, but it was frustrating for many others who wondered if that was all the culture that was left. The advertising campaign was abandoned. ☐ From bus windows, visiting school children look out at a sawmill, administrative offices, a hydroelectric facility, and a fish hatchery. They might stay with a Warm Springs family in a modern home well-stocked with video games and soda pop. Invariably, one of the students will remark with disappointment, "I thought Indians lived in tepees!" ☐ And what of the young medical intern who spends two years on the reservation answering his pager or his doorbell at all hours? He knows people by their stab wounds, their diabetes-ravaged legs, or their children lost to car wrecks. Perhaps he has not had time to feast with the people at the longhouse or bathe with them in the sweathouses. ☐ It is common for people who come to Warm Springs with a nostalgic image of the Indian to leave pronouncing the culture dead. They see "remnants"—perhaps a bit of paid pageantry or a half-hearted beadwork demonstration—and they feel pity. Or they see the collision of white and Indian culture—a pop can flying out the window of a pickup overflowing with kids and powwow music—and they feel anger. What they do not stay long enough to see is the undercurrent of culture that still flows beneath these layers of

visible loss. Deep-rooted religious and cultural traditions still offer solace and a sense of pride to many tribal members seeking refuge from the confusion of the twentieth century or simply wanting to celebrate their Indianness. Yes, there are certain gaps in their cultural memories and disagreements over ritual. But the people of Warm Springs do not play at being Indian; there is a real continuity of customs and beliefs from the last century despite the interruption in their life-style.

It is just this proximity to the last century that is often overlooked when outsiders view life on the Warm Springs Reservation. When they see a longhouse ceremony interrupted by undisciplined children or a meeting set for seven o'clock starting at eight, they are looking at a people in the throes of a cultural transition that began only 130 years ago. That may seem to be plenty of time for full assimilation; after all, it is argued, immigrant families from all over the world have blended with American culture in a generation's time. But when a tribal hunting and gathering culture that has adapted for thousands of years to a specific set of environmental factors abruptly encounters and is surrounded forcibly by a culture entering the Machine Age, it is too great a leap to be made gracefully.

The transition might have been smoother if the tribes had not been removed to an isolated reservation, unable to evolve naturally in contact with white culture. After the initial shock of removal, the tribes were in a state of cultural suspension while reservation bureaucrats and teachers coaxed them to adopt the ways of a culture that was distant and irrelevant. Considering the low value that was placed on their own culture, and the distorted view they were getting of white culture, it is a wonder that the people retained any sense of identity at all.

Now the people try to reconcile visions of a future symbolized by the high-heeled owner of a split-level home whose children are college-bound, and the moccasined old woman digging her last roots and hoping she taught her songs well enough to her granddaughter. A lucky minority are able to carry the songs inside them while they go about their eight-to-five routines; they have found that agreeable spot where the cultures join, a serene synthesis of values. Many more find themselves at war with themselves and with each other as they feel pressured to choose between the cultures.

But the undercurrent is there. Warm Springers do not have to be longhouse regulars to feel the cultural bond that ties them together. The tension created by competing ways of life on the reservation actually provides a kind of ongoing dialogue as the Tribes decide their future. Few tribal members would maintain that either the "old ways" or the "white man's ways" represent the only way. Instead, there seems to be a tacit understanding that, while economic and political strength will ensure the Tribes' physical survival, cultural strength will give them a reason to survive.

THE EARTH MOVES

As traders, the Wasco and Sahaptin people were accustomed to the influence of new people, new ideas, and new ways. They welcomed a variation in a ritual, a different way to prepare food, or the introduction of new blood into their groups. But their culture evolved slowly during the thousands of years they inhabited the Columbia River drainage; their life-style was so well-suited to the environment that there was little pressure to change. The only upheavals the people were likely to have experienced were from restless mountains and rampaging rivers.

The coming of white people was not unlike such a natural cataclysm. It swirled in around the native culture, breaking it up and changing it forever. But, like the mountains and rivers in their normal state, the first whites were benign; it was not until their numbers swelled and their thirst for the resources grew that the rumblings and rising waters of cultural conflict became increasingly destructive.

There is reason to believe that the Plateau culture was changing in response to white presence in the West even before the new race actually arrived on the Columbia. Pressures on the perimeter of their territory may have been responsible in part for the intensification of the role of prophecy and the development of new religious expressions during the late eighteenth

century; and faraway conflicts may have caused a subtle pulling together of the autonomous bands and villages of Plateau people to create a more tribal or federation identity. But such changes, difficult to document in the pre-history period, probably represented a more gradual cultural evolution than what was to come later.

The earth didn't really move under the Sahaptin, Wasco, and Paiute cultures until the tribes were removed to the reservation. It was then that their traditional ways of governing, worshipping, eating, dressing, speaking, and even conducting their family life came under the closest scrutiny of the new culture and were found wanting.

The people of the reservation wanted very much to be cooperative, but their own ancient laws spoke to them as strongly as those of the white man. This conflict of values is expressed in a poignant statement made by Chief Mark of the Wascos almost fifteen years after his people moved to the reservation.

My heart is warm like fire, but there are cold spots in it. I don't know how to talk. I want to be a white man. My father did not tell me it was wrong to have so many wives. I love all my women . . . I don't know how to do; I want to do right. I am not a bad man. I know your new law is good; the old law is bad. We must be like the white man. I am a man; I will put away the old law . . . I want you to tell me how to do right. I love my women and children. I can't send any of them away; what must I do?*

As the three cultural groups on the reservation struggled with such conflicts and learned to be ashamed of their brown skin and their "uncivilized" ways, they also changed with respect to one another. In the first reservation years, the Sahaptins, Wascos, and Paiutes lived fairly separately—at Simnasho, Agency, and Seekseequa respectively. When the boarding school

opened and the commissary and other conveniences began to appear at the Agency, there was more mixing. This natural interaction, coupled with the government's tendency to see only two cultural distinctions—white and Indian—served to dilute tribal differences.

Increasingly, Indianness came to be defined in Sahaptin terms, while Wasco and Paiute traditions began slipping into obscurity. The Wascos may have been dominant on the river, but their commercial strength and worldliness also predisposed them to adapting to white culture. Critical of the less sophisticated Sahaptin people, who clung more fiercely to their traditions, the Wascos let the details of their own traditions slip away and they ironically came to identify with their neighbors on cultural matters. The Paiutes, who were greatly outnumbered on the reservation and were isolated from their Great Basin relatives, easily gave way to Sahaptin traditions. While this consolidation of culture marked a real loss for the Wascos and Paiutes, it may have ensured that some culture would survive.

Even before the reservation was established, the Plateau and Basin cultures experienced an infusion of Plains traditions. Probably with the increased mobility brought by the horse, such elements of the Plains culture as tepees, buckskin clothing, certain songs and dances, and possibly the drum made their way into the lives of the Northwest peoples. This influence has since been felt nationwide and is especially noticeable at powwows, where regalia and dance styles are heavily Plains-derivative.

While many Warm Springs tribal members today still identify with their ancestral tribes, the lines have blurred with intermarriage, and a surface homogeneity hides the once distinct cultural traditions. Some of the older Wascos and Paiutes on the reservation speak their own languages, but Sahaptin is the language used in the longhouse and when translation is provided at public meetings. There have been attempts made by the Wasco chief to gather his people together to revive and perform Wasco songs and dances, but the group is usually short-lived. Paiute songs, dances, language, and crafts—better preserved among the Nevada tribes—are all but invisible at Warm Springs.

What is left of the Wasco and Paiute traditions to-

---

*A.B. Meacham, *Wigwam and Warpath*. I first saw the quote in Jarold Ramsey, *Coyote Was Going There*.

day is reflected mainly in temperament and values. Wascos have come to be distinguished by a certain sophistication and ambition, as well as a wry, earthy sense of humor that is often evidenced in their story-telling. They are often the entrepreneurs, the college-bound, the ones with many white friends. The Paiutes, a rugged lot like their desert forebears, are stick game players and rodeo cowboys—ready to risk and dare. But even these characterizations are more and more difficult to support.

CHANGING VISIONS

The prophecies about the coming of a light complected people had arisen from a spiritual context that was at once ancient and in flux. Some scholars believe that the spiritual world of the Columbia River tribes changed dramatically in the late eighteenth century, expanding beyond the ancient winter spirit dances to a new expression of prophetic concern with salvation and the hereafter. This "prophet dance," a name coined by Leslie Spier,* may have been aboriginal in origin, but when elements of Christianity began drifting into the Northwest, probably early in the nineteenth century, the natives could not help but be struck by the similarities. According to Spier, the presence of the prophet dance may have caused the river people to be particularly receptive to Christianity.

Elements of Christian, specifically Catholic, ritual are believed to have been brought west by a group of Iroquois Indians visiting the Flathead people in Montana in 1820; from there, the new forms travelled along the trade network to the Columbia. They were easily incorporated into the prophet dance tradition.

By the mid-nineteenth century, an apocalyptic time for the Indians of the West, there was need for new prophecies. White Americans by then were being driven westward by their own religious and cultural conviction that the continent was theirs to settle. They had even created a byword for their foretold expansion, "manifest destiny." For some, the Indian tribes were in the way. For others, the "savages" were ripe for receiving the glories of civilization. With his persistent notion of removal to reservations, backed up by the persuasive presence of the U.S. Army, the white man seemed to portend only cultural or physical death for the Indians.

It was in the lean, despairing first years of reservation life that Indian people turned to their traditional religions with renewed fervor. The words of a few great prophets inspired not only dramatic cultural revivals but also active resistance to the intrusion of white civilization.

In the Pacific Northwest, in the same decade that most of the treaties were made, a prophet named Smohalla arose from obscurity along the upper Columbia River and gave new life to the aboriginal religion of the Sahaptin people. Smohalla (meaning "dreamer") brought back from death the traditional message of the destruction and rebirth of the world, but added a new twist: that the white people would be forever destroyed and only those Indians who followed the traditional ways would be resurrected. To Smohalla and his followers, Earth and its resources had been provided by the Creator to be shared by all inhabitants; it was wrong to parcel it out and cultivate it, and the idea of a reservation was anathema.

In a speech transcribed by Major J.W. MacMurray in 1884, Smohalla said:

'Those who cut up the lands or sign papers for lands will be defrauded of their rights and will be punished by God's anger . . .

'You ask me to plow the ground! Shall I take a knife and tear my mother's bosom? Then when I die she will not take me to her bosom to rest.

'You ask me to dig for stone! Shall I dig under her skin for her bones? Then when I die I cannot enter her body to be born again.

'You ask me to cut grass and make hay and sell it and be rich like white men! But how dare I cut off my mother's hair?

---

* Leslie Spier, *The Prophet Dance of the Northwest and Its Derivatives: The Source of the Ghost Dance.*

166

'. . . My young men shall never work. Men who work cannot dream, and wisdom comes to us in dreams.' *

There had been many prophets before him, but the piquancy of Smohalla's message probably lay in its timing; it ascribed a new relevancy to dying cultural traditions while it unified believers into a final resistance to the white presence. In the Smohalla Cult, which centered on an enhanced prophet dance that invoked a dream-like state, followers found clarity and direction where there had been confusion. Out of the dreams of the dancers came the inspiration for the celebrated defiance of Chief Joseph and the Nez Perce, and the retaliation of the Bannocks against the U.S. Army. The rituals of the modern Washat religion practiced today at Warm Springs and on other Plateau reservations owe their vitality to Smohalla's enhancement of traditional religious forms in the last century.

At the same time in the Great Basin, possibly inspired by the Smohalla Cult, another prophet named Wovoka returned from a visit to the dead with a nearly identical message. The resulting Ghost Dance spread through California and Nevada and east over the Rocky Mountains. There it took on great power among the Sioux, who donned bullet-proof "ghost shirts" to resist the Army.

Smohalla had brought back from the land of the dead very specific ceremonies and tenets based on both native and Christian ritual. Washat beliefs today reflect the same harmonious blend of elements. It may never be known to what degree aboriginal beliefs paralleled Christian tenets or were influenced by them, but the Washat worshipers themselves say their people have always believed in one Creator and the resurrection of the human spirit. Stories of the creation of man and woman, a great flood, and the after-life are strikingly similar to biblical stories. But also at the core of the Washat religion is a reverence for the earth and its

inhabitants, all set in motion by a Creator. The aboriginal notion of spirits in all things may now be more symbolic of God's omnipresence than it is a literal explanation of the natural make-up of the world. Good is defined in terms of respect for the earth, the elders, and traditional Indian values, leaving it up to each person to live according to the best Indian impulses in order to find his or her way into the "golden world."

The Washat religion is a cultural rallying point for the people of Warm Springs. Believers of other traditional religions, even Baptists and Presbyterians, seek refuge in the reservation's longhouses and find enough commonality in beliefs to inspire fellowship. Strangers, too, are welcome in the longhouse, where they can experience a ceremony much like this:

The sweet scent of salmon and roots floats out from the kitchen as the drummers start their last set of seven songs. The songs, divinely given and passed down from generation to generation, speak of reverence for the earth, visions of the spirit world to come, and the power of the Creator. The seven drummers at the west end of the longhouse beat their hand drums slowly, the bell-ringer shakes her hand bell, and a single voice begins the song, to be joined by the other six voices. Washat means "worship dance," so to sing is not enough. Young dancers—the boys in ribbon shirts and the girls in wingdresses, both wearing moccasins and holding eagle feathers—have fallen into two opposite lines. For the first verse they mark time with their bodies, then the tempo picks up and they move as one, counterclockwise around the longhouse. Worshippers on the north and south benches sing quietly, their hands moving in prayerful arcs away from their hearts. The song builds, the air is thick with the drumbeat and plaintive voices, legs ache, and suddenly the song is over, to a chorus of "a-a-a-i," amen. Between songs, feathers flutter to cool the hot, moist faces; an elder stands before the drummers, and, her voice breaking, offers prayer and testimony; people talk quietly; the ovens are checked. When the seventh set of songs is completed on this Sunday morning, the people will eat together and give thanks.

*James Mooney, "The Ghost Dance Religion and the Sioux Outbreak of 1890."

167

Bell-ringer Matilda Mitchell leads worship songs at a Sunday Washat service at the Simnasho Longhouse. Sometimes it is hard to get the full complement of seven drummers, but the construction of a new, larger longhouse in 1985 was one indication that the traditional religion is far from dead. (Cynthia D. Stowell)

Washat ritual permeates life at Warm Springs, providing a framework for most traditional activities on the reservation, such as feasts, funerals, name-givings, and first kills. Washat prayer songs are offered at all manner of public gatherings, from community dinners to building dedications. Although present on other Plateau reservations, the Washat religion is completely decentralized. Each longhouse has its own leader, usually a respected elder who has inherited the position and is a teacher and spiritual guide as well as the worship director.

Tribal Council underwrites some longhouse functions, particularly in the area of food supplies. At feast time, designated rootdiggers, berry pickers, fishermen, or hunters provide the principal foods, but the Tribal Council also buys salmon from local fishermen to stock the longhouse freezers, and allocates money for feasts and funerals. Such Council support has become necessary with the change from a subsistence economy to a forty-hour-a-week, wage-earning economy; people no longer have time to gather enough traditional foods for communal, ceremonial purposes.

Out of the cultural confusion that characterized the early reservation period arose two other noteworthy spiritual movements on Northwest reservations. The Shaker and Feather religions, both of which have followers on the Warm Springs Reservation today, grew out of the same tension between Indian and white cultures that had created the Smohalla Cult. The Shakers incorporated a great deal of Christian ritual while the Feather sect signaled a return to native healing forms, but both movements had roots in ancient shamanistic traditions.

Of the many spiritual customs and rituals practiced by Indian groups, shamanism was probably the most feared and scorned by white observers. Medicine men had contact with a spirit world that Christians felt was associated with Satan. Shamanism was greatly discouraged by reservation officials, but it never died out. Indian "doctoring" remained a popular, if covert, way of treating physical and psychological ills. Shakers, while they are apt to denounce shamanism, seem to have taken this impulse for spiritual healing and combined it with Christian doctrine to make a sect that was more palatable to non-Indians and still satisfying to Indians.

The Indian Shaker phenomenon (which is unrelated to Ann Lee and the Shakers of the East coast) had its start around Puget Sound in the 1880s, when a Skokomish man named John Slocum "died" and came back to life with a message for Indian people—a familiar prophetic motif for Northwest tribes. A logger who had gambled and indulged in other vices, Slocum had been told by an angel that he was unfit for Heaven and was sent back to earth to teach other Indians how to live good lives and gain entry to Heaven. Slocum associated evil with gambling, horse racing, the use of tobacco and alcohol, and the practice of shamanism. To ward off such sinful behavior, Slocum asked his potential converts to accept the Word of God not as it was presented in the Bible but through revelation, and he introduced such Roman Catholic rituals as kneeling, making the sign of the cross, lighting candles, ringing bells, and wearing vestments.

Some time after Slocum's preaching began, he be-came seriously ill and his wife Mary received the gift and power of shaking—the trembling of hands and body upon which Shaker worship and healing are now centered. The new religion spread quickly around the Sound, north into British Columbia, and south into Oregon and northern California. At Warm Springs, the Shaker religion has been particularly popular among the Wasco people, perhaps because of their closer identification with coastal culture or their tendency to bridge the gap between white and Indian cultures. But the bell in the steeple of their cinder block church along Shitike Creek calls individuals from all three tribes to worship services on Sunday morning or healings on Saturday night. Shakers often have altars (prayer tables with ritual candles and bells) in their homes and healings are frequently done at home. Non-Shakers sometimes ask Shakers to "work on" them when they are feeling "sick in the Indian way;" even the late leader of the Feather religion sought help from the Shakers when his own proteges were unable to cure him.

Non-Indian visitors to the Shaker Church are much less common than to the longhouse, but the seriously interested are admitted and are encouraged to participate as much as is comfortable in a ceremony like this one:

Inside the church, all is white. White crosses bearing white candles hang on white walls. Men with white T-shirts and women wearing white dresses and shoes kneel before a white prayer table, voicing individual prayers that rise and swell. It is a cacophony of white noise. When the last "In the name of the Father, the Son and the Holy Ghost" is intoned, in English and Nisqually, a chair is placed before the prayer table and a woman in a white dress is seated. Men take large hand bells from the table, women hold glowing candles, and a song begins. It is a simple, but haunting tune reminiscent of traditional Indian songs, Gregorian chants, and southern gospels. The deep-throated bells clang steadily, the worshippers' feet tramp heavily on the wooden floor, and the song repeats and builds un-

169

The Indian Shaker religion was initially very popular among the Wascos. Followers who assembled for this 1905 photograph were, from left to right: (back row) Bill Thomas, Arthur Symentire, Davis Miller, Peter Brunoe, Cain Brunoe, Mrs. Jake Snioups, Susan Brunoe, Eva Brunoe, Jeanette Brunoe, Lorraine Brunoe. (Photograph by Harry Miller, Sr. and Gillis Dizney, Dan Macy Collection)

til the church reverberates, its suspended crosses swaying, its candles flickering. Inside the church on the warm, buzzing summer evening, the people generate white heat. Lifting their faces and their open palms heavenward, they wander trance-like, eyes closed, but never colliding; they warm their hands on the candle flames and touch one another; from the air, one receives a spirit, clasping his hands around it, struggling, and flinging it upward; one person begins shaking, her hands first, then her head and torso. Healing hands are laid on the seated woman; they brush away spirits or scoop them up and toss them away; flame-warmed hands smooth and pat the woman to restore her own spirit; some hands stroke the cross at the table and carry the gathered strength to the woman. Eventually, the song subsides to a moan, the tramping and the ringing stop, the exhausted Shakers sit, and the healed woman rises to testify. Many hours later the worshipers close their service by filing around the room three times, treading lightly, each person brushing the open palm of every other person. Stepping into the cool night air, their ears ring, their feet throb, their hearts pound, and they are contented.

There is no formal membership in the Shaker church but there is some bureaucracy. The Warm Springs parish elects officers, exists as part of the larger Northwest-wide church organization, and adheres to the official articles of incorporation drawn up in Washington in 1910. Shaker doctrine is left somewhat vague to allow for interpretation by individuals, who are encouraged to act according to their own consciences and to use their imaginations in creating new ritual elements. Yet Shakers do share a belief in one God as manifest in the Trinity, the struggle of good and evil, the inherent sinfulness of humans, immortality of the soul, and a final judgment. Because of their close contact with the world of spirits, Shakers have also cultivated the extrasensory ability to locate lost objects or people and have been known to cooperate with the tribal police in searches and investigations.

Early disenchantment with the Shaker religion led to a third prophecy and the subsequent growth of the Feather Cult, an ecstatic, healing sect that eschews the Christian trappings of Shakerism and embraces the traditional Indian values of the longhouse people. It was a Shaker living near the present community of Hood River along the Columbia River, a man named Jake Hunt, to whom the Feather religion was revealed around the turn of the century. After Shaker rituals had failed to save several members of his family, Hunt became very despondent and vengeful. But, during a profound sleep, he had a vision that showed him a new way. A bright disk of light appeared to him and from this light came a voice instructing him about the drums, eagle feathers, and songs that were to be the symbols of the new religion. With his new name—Nashat Ticham ("Earth Moves")—the convert took this information back to his Shaker friends and built a tule reed longhouse on the Washington side of the river, calling on God to cause earthquakes everywhere except on the site of the longhouse, as a sign to skeptical people.

The Feather Cult did not spread as widely as the prophecies of Slocum and Smohalla, but quietly grew among the people of the Columbia and their relatives on the Yakima, Umatilla, and Warm Springs reservations. Much of the knowledge of Feather ritual and beliefs at Warm Springs has resided with one elderly man (now deceased), at whose home the services were held until he died in 1986. Feather believers, many of whom also participate in Washat services, gathered in the ceremonial wing of this man's house on the Deschutes River for healings, feasts, and celebrations of other life events, often staying for several days at a time. They are also invited to people's homes to perform their healing ritual.

The house was open to all, the first visit usually by personal invitation. One day, when his daughters are ready to carry on, the house may again fill with energy, as on this night:

"Sack 'em up," says the old man. The drummers bundle up their hand drums and sticks, and the Washat service is over. At the east end of his ceremonial room, the old man in Western clothes and gray braids pulls his eagle feathers off the wall and a different kind of music begins—simpler, more hypnotic, accompanied by a single drum or pounding stick. A tired woman with a lame leg is seated before him, and the old man gathers his helpers around. Together, dance-like, the healers surround the woman, brushing and stroking her with flicking eagle feathers. Into their cupped hands they take bad spirits, struggle with them, and toss them into the air. More troublesome spirits will cause the healers to stagger, fall, or vomit. The song goes on and on, as the healers move rhythmically around the woman. She smiles faintly, her face uplifted. The people standing along the walls sing, louder and louder, working themselves into an ecstatic state. One woman starts to spin and a circle forms around her to break her fall as she spins faster and faster. It will be a long night, with many people healed and many songs sung. Water and snacks are brought around, and people step outside to breathe the cool air by the river. Later, the old man gives away blankets, shawls, wingdresses, and shirts and he talks about his long association with the Feather religion. The dancing begins again. Exhaustion is greeted and passed. The old man is pleased: he has come of age as a teacher and his people are learning.

Even at the Feather services, which are so unlike Christian worship, the people invoke God and Jesus, display crosses from time to time, and denounce smoking and drinking like the best fundamentalist Christians. The religion brought by the settlers and missionaries clearly held much appeal for the native people along the Columbia. What is most interesting is that aboriginal religion and Christianity actually joined to resist the more intrusive elements of white culture, to anchor the people during violent cultural upheaval.

Christianity by itself was somewhat less successful in offering the reservation people the hope they needed to survive. The Presbyterian church, which established a mission at Warm Springs in 1874, is still a presence in the community today, though it has a

Membership in the Warm Springs Presbyterian Church has always been small, as in this photograph from the early 1900s, but the church is remembered for its food and clothing assistance during hard times. (Photograph by Harry Miller, Sr. and Gillis Dizney, Dan Macy Collection.)

lower profile than it had in its early years. From the start, students at the boarding school were required to attend services and lessons at the Presbyterian Church, thus creating both resentment and affection for the institution. On more than one occasion, the church kept starvation at bay by supplementing inadequate government rations. A couple of well-liked ministers put in long careers at the Warm Springs Church, but in recent years turnover has been high, the congregation has tended to be more non-Indian than local, and the church has struggled with its proper role in the community. Even so, some members have been trying to revitalize the Presbyterian Church that existed for many years at Simnasho.

The much younger Baptist Church, with a similarly small congregation, has attracted proportionately more Indian members, partly because of a popular pastor who, with his family, has made the reservation his home for the last few decades. It is possible, too,

that the people's affinity for the ecstatic and testimonial elements of religion makes them comfortable with the more fundamental of the Christian sects. The Full Gospel Church in Warm Springs, guided by a tribal member, draws a broad cross section of the community to its periodic revivals and tent meetings.

The Roman Catholic church, which found many converts among Midwestern and Plains tribes as well as other tribes in the Northwest, did not figure into the largely Protestant missionary efforts along the Columbia River, though some Catholic ritual was passed westward along with buffalo robes. But a small group of loyal worshippers maintain a Catholic chapel in Warm Springs, visited on Sunday by a priest from Madras. Rounding out the diverse religious picture at Warm Springs are a few practicing Mormons, Jehovah's Witnesses, and members of the peyote-using Native American Church.

The Warm Springs people's rather generous, or

172

perhaps relaxed, view of religion is best reflected in their funerals, where representatives of all reservation faiths are invited to offer solace or inspiration to family and friends. It is not inconceivable for one death to prompt Shaker services at home, overnight ceremonies at the longhouse, an open casket service at a church, and a traditional burial with remarks from all sects. This is not to say that some rivalry or exclusiveness does not exist among the reservation religions. It is just that these differences can be overlooked when there is a greater purpose to be served. Few would challenge the assertion that it is the same God to which the reservation's many believers turn.

THE PROMISE OF EDUCATION

While new religious forms were giving the Warm Springs people some measure of hope and strength, the haphazard establishment of schooling on the reservation was a source of great disappointment. One of the selling points in the treaty had been the promise of education, which at least two of the chiefs at the treaty council felt was a key to their people's future. Said Kuck-up, as recorded in the treaty council minutes, "When our children learn to read and write, I[t] will be the same as bringing them to light . . . We have been asleep and just waked up when we could read and write." No doubt they felt they would be at a better advantage with the white man if they were fluent in English. But it was clear from remarks made by Superintendent Palmer that the government had something more in mind. In reviewing the services and provisions promised by the president in exchange for the land, Palmer said, "You will soon be able to live like white people." The educational system devised by the BIA took that notion very seriously.

The first schoolhouse, a day school, had appeared at the Agency by 1862, but it was so poorly built that it was unfit for use in the cold seasons. Attendance was low and irregular, not only because of inadequate facilities but because of the distances students had to travel, the departure of families from the reservation for traditional food gathering, and rampant illness. The first boarding school was completed in the early 1870s,

but it was too small from the outset and was soon in disrepair. During the next two decades, the school functioned sporadically, hampered by overcrowding, leaks and drafts, and a lack of supplies. Few people on the reservation today remember that there was also a succession of day and boarding schools at Simnasho, serving North End children through the sixth grade, until the last building burned down around the turn of the century. When the reservation schools were not functioning, some older students were sent to the Oregon Indian School in Forest Grove, west of the Cascade Mountains, where the wet climate disagreed with the children and further weakened their resistance to illness.

Even in 1897, when sturdy dormitories and classrooms finally were constructed at the Agency and education was made compulsory, only about half the school-age children on the reservation attended regularly. It is just as well; the school could not have accommodated them all anyway. Clearly, education did not have an auspicious start at Warm Springs.

Boarding school was an unhappy, wrenching experience for the community. Children were separated from their families, often for the first time, and allowed to go home only for the summer and for holidays that did not coincide with the Indian culture's meaningful times. The children's long black hair was shorn and they were forbidden to speak their native languages. They conformed to a military regimen, complete with parading, drills, and morning and evening flag ceremonies. The style of teaching was very formal, with the traditional Anglo subjects presented in a rigid classroom atmosphere. This method was completely foreign to children who had learned the skills and values they needed for adult life through observing and imitating their elders and listening to their stories.

Beyond classroom time, girls spent long hours sewing, cooking, and house cleaning, and boys put in time at the dairy barn, blacksmith shop, and parade grounds. Old photographs of students uncomfortably dressed in starched pinafores, Lord Fauntleroy suits, and military uniforms reveal a certain reluctance, even a sadness, that matched their parents' resistance to the school that had come to dominate life in Warm Springs.

173

Reservation boarding schools like the one at Warm Springs were at the heart of the government's efforts to assimilate Indians into white culture. Native clothing, hairstyles, and language were forbidden and families gave up much of their child-rearing functions to white teachers and matrons. (Photograph by Harry Miller, Sr. and Gillis Dizney, Dan Macy Collection)

It was a mutual dissatisfaction felt by the parents and the government officials. In an 1890 letter to the Commissioner of Indian Affairs in Washington, D.C., Agent J.C. Luckey complained that Indian adults were interfering with the educational process:

> The old Indians make daily visits to the Agency and are a great annoyance in the school as they converse with the children (especially the boys) in their native tongue and some of them endeavor to prejudice the children against the school as most of the older Indians oppose education and their children have to be brought into school by a police.*

---

*A copy of this letter is in the possession of the Confederated Tribes.

The boarding school represented a very thorough effort at "civilizing," from the arguably humane delousing treatments to the irrelevant lessons in etiquette and the staff's refusal to acknowledge any value in Indian culture. Although the regimen relaxed somewhat and the content of the curriculum was updated through the years, the mission of the school remained the same until it was absorbed by the local school district in 1961 and the dormitories closed in 1967. People in their forties tell the same stories their parents and grandparents tell about having their braids cuts, being punished for speaking their own language, and learning from the disdain of teachers and administrators to feel shame for their Indianness.

In the minds of many people associated with Warm Springs, the boarding school is responsible in

large measure for the breakdown of the traditionally strong Indian family. Parents and grandparents who lost control over their children for the better part of each year had little opportunity to establish their authority, impart moral and ethical values, or teach traditional survival skills. The children in turn had no consistent role models to guide them when they became parents themselves. After several generations of this usurpation of parenting responsibilities, the reservation family—though now back together physically—is unsure of itself. Parents discipline tentatively, if at all, and children are confused about what values to embrace.

By sending some of the better students to finish up at off-reservation schools, the boarding school system was also teaching youngsters not to excel. "A lesson not lost on the other students was not to be too successful in any number of achievements or one might be sent farther away from home," wrote Janice White Clemmer in her 1980 doctoral dissertation about education at Warm Springs in the nineteenth century. Clemmer is a tribal member who overcame the fear of excelling and went on to earn two doctorates, a first for an Indian woman.

It is not surprising after this ninety-year experience with the boarding school that the Warm Springs community today is ambivalent about the value of education. Parents continually express their support for public education, but this attitude is not successfully communicated to their children, who tend to fall behind the national averages after the first two years of grade school. While a century ago parents made their dislike of the boarding school plain, a more subtle but similar statement is made today when regular attendance at school loses out to cultural and family activities, such as powwows, rootdigging, or caring for younger siblings.

If the classroom experience were more rewarding for Warm Springs students, family priorities might be different. But education, now the responsibility of Jefferson County School District 509-J, is still dominated by Anglo values, both in the content of the curriculum and the style of teaching. While most tribal members would agree that the reservation's young people need to acquire the modern skills required to operate their tribal enterprises and government, they also feel that the ways the white culture has chosen to teach those skills have made them difficult to learn. Teachers have trouble understanding their reserved, non-competitive Indian students who find it difficult to be verbal and embarrassing to be singled out.

These differences become critical when Indian students leave the relative homogeneity of Warm Springs Elementary to attend the sixth through twelfth grades in Madras, where they are outnumbered by white students two-to-one. Some Indian teenagers come out of their protected corners with their fists up while others direct their physical prowess into team sports; some withdraw into alcohol and drugs while others mix easily with white students. But nearly all are behind academically when they get to Madras and it takes some extra effort, from students and staff alike, to catch up. Many never do; Warm Springs students comprise only about ten percent of the graduating seniors, though they are about one-third of the junior high population.

With the help of federal programs, the school district has been able to address the Indian students' special needs more successfully in the last decade. Title IV of the Indian Education Act of 1972 supplemented the Indian Welfare (Johnson-O'Malley) Act of 1934 to provide more services to Indian children in public schools. Indian counselors, tutors, community liaisons, and coursework in Indian history and language were brought into the 509-J school system with such federal funds. When Indian high school students continued to fail, the school district worked with the Tribes in 1979 to open an alternative day school (housed coincidentally in the former boys' dormitory of the boarding school) that provided a relaxed, individualized learning environment with a career orientation. After two years, the school district assumed full responsibility for the program.

In 1985, the Tribes, the BIA, and the school district signed an agreement to coordinate "in perpetuity" those services and programs benefiting tribal children. While this stole some thunder from years of rumors about the Tribes operating their own school system, the Tribes clearly have begun exercising more control

175

Not much has changed in the rootdigger's work through the centuries. Using an iron kapn *(digging stick) instead of the traditional wooden one, Viola Kalama unearths* piyaxi *(bitterroot) for a contemporary April Root Feast. (Cynthia D. Stowell)*

over the education of tribal members, from establishment of their own early childhood programs to greater involvement in adult education and career training. A community learning center that was proposed by the Tribes in 1985 would consolidate all these programs into one large complex of buildings; intriguingly, the architect's model indicates elementary classrooms as well.

In 1958, the reservation's first college degree was awarded. By 1986, forty-eight tribal members had bachelor, master's, and doctoral degrees, many earned with the help of the tribal-BIA scholarship program, which pays tuition and expenses if a minimum grade point average is maintained. The Minors' Trust Fund, a savings account set up for each enrolled child and fed with his first eighteen years of per capita payments, was designed to pay college expenses but is more often spent on new cars, stereos, or good times. But in

176

a show of support for higher education, tribal voters in 1986 authorized the Tribes to set aside six million dollars to carry the scholarship program into the twenty-first century.

THE EARTH'S GIFTS TO THE PEOPLE

The image of the rootdigger bending to earth perfectly symbolizes the Warm Springs people's traditional bond to the earth and the foods it produces. Although the people no longer depend on native foods for their physical survival, they still celebrate the roots, berries, salmon, and venison as gifts from a Creator who intends for the Indian people to survive as a culture. The ritual gathering, serving, and eating of the traditional foods is more than a thanksgiving; it is a cultural affirmation. As the salmon of the Columbia dwindle, as root fields give way to grazing or farmland, and as huckleberries are coveted by non-Indians, the Warm Springs culture is certainly threatened.

The annual first-food celebrations, which formally sanction the harvest of certain plants and animals, express most eloquently the importance of native foods to the people. When the people still lived on the river, the salmon feast in late spring was the biggest celebration; the arrival of the spring chinook is still marked by the few who live along the river with a feast at Celilo Village, drawing participants from the Warm Springs, Yakima, and Umatilla reservations, and many non-reservation Indians. But at Warm Springs, the principal first-food observances are the root and huckleberry feasts, with a lesser feast for the wild celery.

Root Feast is a springtime celebration of three plants native to central Oregon. Few non-Indians know the roots are there, a boon to the Indians since they do not have to compete for them. The only problem is finding their favorite off-reservation digging spots fenced in and posted with "no trespassing" signs by landowners. Rootdiggers have made agreements with some ranchers, but have failed or not even tried to gain the cooperation of others.

Many people on the reservation can remember going out to the root fields by horse and wagon and camping out for several days until their bags were full.

It was a time of hard work and festivity for whole families. Now the women pack their children and a lunch into a four-wheel-drive for the day, perhaps overnight if it is a distant field. But the method of digging the roots has changed little; the gently curved wooden stick (*kapn*) of the last century is now made of wrought iron, but the scouting, walking, stooping, and unearthing have never changed.

Beginning in April each year, the sharp eyes of the Warm Springs women scan the rocky ground for the telltale signs of three small plants that most people would not notice: a tiny bunch of bright green succulent spears; a taller, lacy-leafed plant with crowns of white flowers and papery seeds; or a waving cluster of spherical yellow flowers. In Sahaptin, they are *piyaxi* (*Lewisa rediviva* or bitterroot), which has a long, spidery root; *luksh* (*Lomatium canbyi*), with a round, bulbous root; and *xoush* (*Lomatium cous*), closely related to luksh but with a more elongated, irregular bulb. All three plants are commonly found on the reservation, but people often go to the Prineville area, fifty miles east of Warm Springs, for the xoush.

On the Thursday before the feast, the cool spring wind is usually whipping the clean scent of sage across Webster Flat. A cluster of women in wingdresses, moccasins, and windbreakers hunch over the dry earth, probing the rocks and brush with the kapns. When each has pried her first spidery or bulbous harvest from the earth, the group stops and sings a prayer song and the ritual digging begins in earnest. Longhouse-appointed diggers work the rest of the day, filling many *wapas* (hip bags) with piyaxi, luksh, and xoush for the Sunday feast. Back at the longhouse, the women and their families peel the thin brown skins off the roots until their fingers are raw, while their men are out fishing and hunting to provide meat for the celebration.

On the morning of the feast, the roots are boiled in huge pots on the longhouse stoves while the venison is roasting in the ovens and the salmon is baking on an outside grill. When the last Washat song is sung, the rootdiggers, fishermen, and hunters take up their gathered food and carry it around the longhouse, setting it before their friends and guests who are seated

at tule mats on the floor. As the name of each food is called out—*Waikanash* (salmon)! *Winat* (venison)! *Xnit* (roots)! *Tmaanit* (berries)!—the people eat tiny ritual portions. "*Choosh!*" is the call for a purifying sip of water and the signal to dig family-style into the bowls of food. Now the hearty eating and socializing begins, while more food is brought out—potatoes, bread, salads, candy, cake, and even Easter eggs, if the two holidays happen to coincide. Full and contented, the people rise and face east for a final prayer song. The roots have been blessed, the Creator has been thanked, and families are now free to gather the sacred food for their own use.

At home, the women might cook the piyaxi fresh, usually by boiling it with bits of salmon, or dry it in the sun to be boiled later. Luksh and xoush are boiled whole or ground into a kind of gruel; ground luksh is shaped into small cakes which are pressed flat and dried in the sun to make snacks called *lukshmi*. Xoush is sometimes dried whole and eaten as a snack.

Root Feast is a greatly anticipated event marking the return of fresh foods to the diet and signaling the end of winter. The women sew new wingdresses* for the feast; many families hold memorial dinners for loved ones who have died in the preceding year so they can be free to participate in the digging and feasting. Root Feast is also the time when legend-telling stops; traditionally, winter was the only season when the people had time to tell stories.

Two other native foods, huckleberries and wild celery, are celebrated with feasts on the reservation. One kind of wild celery, *latitlatit* (*Lomatium grayi*), is the object of a late winter feast, a quiet, private event virtually unknown to the non-Indian public. A late-spring variety of wild celery, *xamsi* (*Lomatium nudicaule*), is valued for its tall, pungent-tasting stalk.

The huckleberry feast held at the HeHe Longhouse in August has a much different tone, because of the universal popularity of huckleberries and easy access to HeHe from Highway 26 and Portland. In fact, the huckleberry (*wiwanu*) is the one native food, other than salmon, for which the Warm Springs people must compete with non-Indians. The sweet blueberry-like fruit is picked primarily off the reservation around Mount Hood in Oregon and Mount Adams and Mount St. Helens in Washington; many berry patches were destroyed by volcanic eruptions of St. Helens, thus increasing competition at the other sites. The August feast is in some ways more like the old celebrations—a weekend-long event complete with powwow dancing and a rodeo. Some people still set up tepees at the HeHe Longhouse during the week before the feast, venturing out to pick berries or staying around camp to enjoy the cool forest air and the cold water of the Warm Springs River. Non-Indians are invited to share in any feast, but the berry feast is more apt to turn into a spectacle, with non-Indians gawking, talking rudely, and even complaining when the free dinner is not served promptly. The frequently heard appeal from the elders is, "This is our church. Please respect it."

First kill and first digging ceremonies further celebrate the native foods but also mark a kind of coming of age for Warm Springs children. At the longhouse, skits are acted out and stories told about the child's successful deer hunting or rootdigging, and the family holds a giveaway to honor the child and thank friends and relatives for support.

Other edible plants gathered on the reservation include several more varieties of roots, chokecherries, black lichen, and medicinal plants and herbs. A popular root found close to the timber is camas (*wakamu*), a bulb that is usually pit-roasted. Other native plants resembling carrots, potatoes, and onions are also dug from reservation soils. One bit of vegetation that the Indians unquestionably have to themselves is the black lichen that hangs from the branches of pine and fir trees. *Kunsh* (*Bryoria fremonti*) is pulled off the trees, cleaned, and roasted, like camas, in a pit filled with hot rocks and layers of pine boughs, dry pine needles, and skunk cabbage leaves. The lichen solidifies into a rubbery cake which is eaten as is or dried and ground up for a dessert pudding eaten with sugar and sometimes raisins. Chokecherries (*tmash*), the last ritual food

---

*A wingdress is a T-shaped, open-sleeved fabric dress tied at the neck with ribbons, belted at the waist, and worn over a long-sleeved underdress. It probably represents a melding of Columbia, Plains and white styles.

178

Gillnets and motorboats have replaced dipnets and scaffolds as the principal means of catching salmon and steelhead on the Columbia River. Fishing seasons on the tamed river are set by the states of Oregon and Washington. (Cynthia D. Stowell)

served at feasts, are found by the rivers and streams on the reservation and elsewhere, and are eaten fresh, canned, or dried and ground for snack cakes.

☐

Most sacred of the native foods is salmon, a migratory fish that for eons encountered only dipnets, spears, and traps on its journey up the Columbia River and the tributaries to its spawning grounds.* But since the white settlers took an interest in the rivers and their resources, the salmon have had to contend with fish wheels, gillnets, and concrete dams, suffering

---

* Three main species of salmon—chinook, sockeye (blueback), and coho (silver)—frequent the Columbia River on a seasonal basis, hatching in fresh water, migrating to the ocean and returning upstream several years later to spawn and die. Steelhead, also valued by the Indians, is a migratory trout similar in flavor to the salmon.

great declines in their populations. Now, where there was once plenty and trade flourished peacefully, Indian fishermen launch their motorboats and dip their nets into rivers of controversy.

Who among the generations of fishermen poised on the rocks with their spears and nets could have guessed that one day the rapids would lie still behind dams and that there would not be enough fish to feed their people or trade to their neighbors? Who could have envisioned courts instead of headmen telling the fishermen when to drop their nets into the river, and the fishermen sitting in jail for doing what their fathers had taught them to do? Who could imagine life without salmon?

Even the treaty, with its provision that the Indians would forever be able to fish "at all usual and accustomed grounds and stations . . . in common with all citizens," could not have anticipated the loss of salmon to generator turbines in four major mainstem dams

and to overzealous ocean harvests. The treaty did, however, consciously remove the river people from their cultural and economic base, and the flooding of Celilo by The Dalles Dam simply completed that separation. For a people whose whole cultural focus was on the catching, preparing, trading, and consuming of fish, the dramatic reduction in the salmon resource is a coda in the long, sad song of cultural demise.

Though only a few Warm Springs men are now dependent on the river for their livelihood, salmon still figures into reservation life in a profound way. It is a central ingredient of every cultural event, served and shared as a way of honoring a person or an occasion. At feasts, salmon itself is honored. Besides its tangible presence in the diet and ceremony of the people, salmon has become a symbol of cultural continuity, of the importance of planning cautiously today so that children and grandchildren may know the taste of the sweet pink meat. It is not just on behalf of the few remaining Warm Springs fishermen that the Tribal Council has fought for treaty fishing rights. It is in the interest of all who value the conservation of the salmon resource and the continuation of tribal culture.

It is a beautiful sight to see a Warm Springs woman turn a silvery thirty-pound salmon into perfect boneless fillets with a few deft strokes of a butcher knife. For special outdoor occasions, or as a matter of course at Kah-Nee-Ta Lodge on weekends, the women will skewer the bright pink fillets on long sticks and lean them over a fire of alder wood in the old way. More often the salmon is wrapped in aluminum foil with oil and salt and baked in an oven. Many people have "dry sheds," where the salmon is hung to dry in the breeze. Dried salmon is eaten like jerky, added to roots or dumplings (*lukameen*), or powdered and used as flavoring, a delicacy called *chlai*. Little of the salmon goes to waste, and the old people especially enjoy the fatty cheeks, oily tail, eyes, and roe.

The harvesting of the salmon and steelhead today would be unrecognizable to the people's ancestors. Now, Indian fishermen put their boats into the Columbia at federally protected "in lieu sites" set aside for the river tribes when the dams were built. They drop their gillnets into the deep water where rocks and thundering falls are only a memory. Commercial fishermen must heed season restrictions set by the Columbia River Compact (the Oregon and Washington fisheries agencies) and enforced by tribal, state, and federal officials. Subsistence fishermen are regulated by the tribal law-and-order code. A few fish go home to the fisherman's families; most are sold to canneries and restaurants for cash, and much of the cash goes right back into fishing gear. Salmon no longer brings wealth, as it did in the days when the daily catch was measured in tons.

During the 1960s, the tribes along the Columbia River, as well as tribes around Puget Sound and throughout the Northwest, began objecting to state regulation of the fishery, which they felt was violating their treaty rights by preventing them from catching their share of the salmon runs. In *United States* v. *Oregon* (1969), U.S. District Court Judge Robert Belloni first affirmed the rights of the treaty tribes by ruling that they were "entitled to a fair share of the fish produced by the Columbia River system."[*] He warned that if no agreement could be reached on a fair share, he would decide, and he retained jurisdiction to protect the rights of the Indians. Judge Belloni also enjoined the state to manage the fishery in such a way that salmon would return to the upriver Indian sites, making it difficult for the state to regulate Indian fishing for any but conservation purposes.

Judge Belloni's decision in *U.S.* v. *Oregon* established the foundation for the decision in *United States* v. *Washington* (1974) by another U.S. District Court Judge, the late George Boldt. Building on the language and intent of Judge Belloni's decision, Judge Boldt ruled that the treaty reference to "fishing in common with the citizens of the United States" should be interpreted as the opportunity to catch fifty percent of the state's off-reservation catch (allowing for escapement for propagation). Judge Belloni then accepted the fifty percent figure used by Judge Boldt and included it in a supplemental order to the decision in *U.S.* v. *Oregon*.

---

[*] The Hon. Robert C. Belloni, *United States of America* v. *State of Oregon*, Civil No. 68–153, Portland, Oregon, April 23, 1969.

180

He urged the states and the tribes to develop comprehensive rules for regulating the fishery without the intervention of the federal court.

In 1977, the states of Oregon and Washington, along with the Columbia River treaty tribes (Warm Springs, Yakima, Umatilla, and Nez Perce) agreed to a five-year allocation plan that included sharing formulas for spring, summer, and fall chinook as well as steelhead, based on fixed escapement goals. At the same time, the four tribes created the Columbia River Intertribal Fish Commission to represent their interests on the river and to generate technical data. The five-year plan took the fishing controversy out of the courts and was cause for some optimism. But problems soon surfaced. The Columbia River Compact consistently overestimated the run sizes, setting seasons for the lower river non-Indian fishermen that invariably created shortfalls in the run above Bonneville Dam in the Indian zone. Indian seasons were then frequently cut off for conservation reasons, and treaty fishermen rarely reached their quota. They began to feel their tribal leaders had "sold out" their treaty rights by agreeing to the plan, and some knowingly violated season restrictions. Meanwhile, the problems of catch monitoring and law enforcement were not being solved and the five-year plan ended in 1982 with no plan to take its place.

The tribes and the states were soon back in court. Tensions increased when a 1982 federal "sting" operation on the river netted over seventy Indian fishermen and charged them with illegally catching and selling salmon. In the course of "Salmonscam," nineteen fishermen were indicted, thirteen convicted, and nine sentenced to prison (including one fisherman from Warm Springs). But, on the positive side, the federal, state, and tribal governments have forged a new law enforcement plan, and as conservation becomes the principal issue, the tribes are finding they have new allies where they previously had only strife. The states and tribes and non-Indian fishermen joined to fight successfully for the U.S.-Canada Pacific Salmon Interception Treaty (1985), which brings the two countries together in management of the ocean fishery (where many Columbia River salmon were being lost before they could start their trip up the river). States and tribes are also working together to implement the fishery mitigation plans of the Northwest Power Planning Act. Almost as a good omen, the combined runs of salmon and steelhead past Bonneville Dam in 1985 were the highest in years (802,000 compared with 392,000 in 1980, according to the Columbia River Intertribal Fish Commission).

With Indian fishermen pitted against commercial and sports fishermen in a bitter struggle for the salmon, the well-publicized "Northwest fishing controversy" degenerated at times into racial conflict. But over time, the reasoned government-to-government approach taken by Warm Springs and the other tribes on behalf of their often angry fishermen has helped to illuminate some legal, ethical, and environmental issues that run deeper than the race to catch the most salmon. Today, there seems to be some sense among the various user groups that without open and rational discussion this could be the salmon's "last stand."

At Sherars Falls on the Deschutes River, about fifty miles north of the reservation, a much smaller fishery attracts both non-Indian sports fishermen and Indian subsistence netters. Here, the people of Warm Springs fish at sites passed down through their families, standing on wooden scaffolds and dipping long-poled nets rhythmically into the cascading water, or waiting for their stationary "set nets" to snare a salmon or steelhead in a back eddy. Downstream, dozens of RVs are parked, their owners sitting on the rock banks patiently minding their poles, which bend infrequently with the weight of a fish. There is a rivalry between the two groups that occasionally erupts in heckling or threats, but there is no commercial interest to sharpen the conflict (other than a few illegal sales by subsistence fishermen). The Confederated Tribes' 1979 purchase of the Sherars site has brought no changes, except for a one-season conservation closure and the presence of a regular tribal police patrol. As long as the salmon and steelhead run at all, a bit of history will live on at Sherars.

Warm Springs is doing what it can to help keep fish runs alive in the Columbia River and its tributaries. In 1978, the Confederated Tribes welcomed a federal fish

Lamprey, commonly called "eels" by Warm Springs gatherers, are there for the taking, even at off-reservation sites such as Willamette Falls on the Willamette River in Western Oregon. The strong oily flavor of eels has not attracted a large non-Indian following. (Cynthia D. Stowell)

hatchery to the Warm Springs River near Kah-Nee-Ta. Using native stock, the hatchery replenishes salmon, steelhead, and trout destined to travel the Columbia, Deschutes, and Warm Springs rivers. The Tribal natural resources department also cooperates with federal and state agencies in tributary habitat studies and fish counts, and the Tribes have become aware of the need to protect spawning streams from the effects of logging, livestock grazing, and other human instrusions.

On both the Columbia and Deschutes rivers, as well as the Willamette River in western Oregon, the people of Warm Springs harvest another river creature, this one virtually ignored by non-Indians. Lampreys, commonly referred to as eels by their pursuers, are plucked from slippery rock faces where they cling with their suction mouths as they wiggle and whip their way upstream to spawn, in the same kind of seasonal migration made by salmon and other anadromous fish. The "eels" are prepared like salmon, either sectioned or filleted and barbecued, baked, or dried, but since

they are so rich and oily, they are used more as a side dish. A treat for some people is the lamprey's notochord, which is dried, and boiled like spaghetti.

The reservation itself continues to be the source of many other useful plants and animals. Venison, traditionally the principal meat in the diet of the river people and some Paiute bands, has always been plentiful until the last few years. Logging and overhunting created a deer shortage that prompted the Tribal Council in 1984 to ban all deer hunting until new seasonal regulations were formulated and enacted later that year. For families accustomed to the year-round hunting, the new restrictions seemed oppressive. But the Council hopes that the closure will alert tribal members to a destructive trend. Spotlight hunting, the off-season killing of does, and the wasting of carcasses all indicate a departure from the traditional respect for the deer and its utility.

Most hunters use the deer responsibly for many of the same purposes as their ancestors. Venison is still served ceremonially in the longhouse and eaten regularly in many homes. While it is not common today for a woman to tan her own deer hides, buckskin is still prized and used widely. Tanning is a laborious process, impressive in its transformation of a rough hide into a luxuriously soft skin. The hide is soaked in water with the deer's brain, then scraped of its hair, stretched on a frame, poked and rubbed with a blunt instrument as it dries, and finally cured in a smokehouse. The smoke-scented buckskin is used for moccasins, gloves, dance and ceremonial regalia, handbags, cradleboard coverings, and other handsewn items. Untanned, the tough and resilient skin is also used for drum heads and parfleches (Indian suitcases of Sioux origin). Bones and antlers from the deer are also used in jewelry and stick game sets.

Each family is also entitled to one elk per year, and as with deer, the elk is used for its meat, hide, and other parts, including a particular pair of teeth used decoratively on powwow outfits. Mink and otter are trapped occasionally for their fur and used in braid wraps. Porcupines, which are often found dead on the roads or highways running through the reservation, give up their hair for dancers' head roaches, and their quills for jewelry.

Certain non-edible plants on the reservation are collected for the manufacture of decorative and utilitarian objects, although the textile arts are fast disappearing. Willow and the bark of cedar roots are gathered for basketry; cattails and a marsh grass called tule are used to make mats for the longhouse. The strong straight trunks of lodgepole pine and young fir make excellent tepee poles.

There are a number of medicinal plants, including field mint ("Indian tea") and juniper berries, that people still utilize, but the few who remember what they are and how they are used are very reluctant to share their knowledge. A few old women still wear small medicine bags around their necks, but they are silent about the contents.

Earth, fire, and water are combined in the sweat bath, a traditional hygienic practice that can be a profound expression of harmony with the earth as well as a spiritual experience. Men and women bathe separately in riverside lodges dug into the earth, carpeted with cedar or fir boughs, and covered with tule or canvas. At the center of the tiny lodge is a fire, tended by an elder or simply the oldest person present, who pours water on the hot rocks to create steam, much like a sauna. In the shadowy glow, the elder tells stories with moral lessons and leads the people in songs, while they sweat out their physical and spiritual impurities. Periodically, bathers leave this cedar-scented sanctuary to plunge into the cold, invigorating river water. While there is hardly a house on the reservation without a modern shower, some of the old people still bathe from time to time in the sweat lodge; it is an opportunity for young and old alike to feel close to the earth, to experience camaraderie, and to cleanse the soul.

STEMMING THE TIDE OF CULTURAL LOSS

Despite the importance of the earth's gifts to the people of Warm Springs, there has been an indisputable drift away from the values and habits shaped by their ancestors' deep involvement with the natural

world. The signs—sometimes very visible, sometimes more subtle—are all around: disposable diapers and beer cans littering Shitike Creek; a pregnant doe slaughtered, the unborn fawns scattered about; popcorn and soda pop swelling and weakening people's bodies; and young people who are more familiar with taverns and television schedules than with their land and the longhouse.

Even when seemingly positive "white" values are embraced, there is a high price to be paid. The eight-to-five workday interferes with the seasonal and daily rhythms that have shaped the culture. Modern homes and private automobiles isolate people from one another and the natural world. Prosperity and demands on people's time encourage a convenience, throwaway mentality. Many people who find the old way of life irrelevant may also fail to take too seriously what the new ways have to offer. Consequently, work attendance and punctuality may not be highly valued; homes and cars tend to fall into disrepair; paychecks are often gone long before the next payday. For some individuals, traditional culture has become nothing more than a reaction to white culture.

And the old people look on sadly. With them resides the culture in its purest forms. They recall days of hard work, frugality, cooperation, and spiritual well-being. But they often keep their secrets to themselves for fear that their precious knowledge of a better way will be misunderstood or exploited. "Why should my grandson, who only likes his video games and motorcycle, learn the song I used to sing when the salmon swam into my net?" an elder might ask. "He would just sell that song and everything I teach him to the white man. I will take what I know to my grave. It is safe there."

On the other hand, so much have some of the older people wanted their children and grandchildren to succeed in a world growing whiter and whiter, that they have shielded them from the language, the longhouse, and the old values while extolling the virtues of a formal education. Whether this is proof of a pragmatic survival impulse or of the deep imprint made by the boarding school, it has nevertheless been a factor in cultural loss.

If young people go to their elders with a serious desire to learn, they are welcome. At the Simnasho Longhouse, the Washat songs are being translated into English for the benefit of an influx of interested young people. The traditional religions still have important socializing functions; the longhouse in particular, since it embraces many aspects of traditional life, from food gathering to coming-of-age rituals, is a real anchor for the old ways.

The most consistent exposure most people on the reservation have to the longhouse is in the context of death and funerals. While the rituals surrounding death are enormously comforting, the longhouse elders feel that if the observance of tradition were a regular part of the people's lives, the community would experience death much less frequently.

As it is, death visits Warm Springs too often. The community reverberates with each passing. It is not hidden from children or spoken of in hushed tones. A notice goes up on the door of Macy's Store and until the deceased's belongings are given away a few days later, the reservation's rhythm is altered; for it is all shared openly.

This time, it is a young father, husband, and rodeo cowboy, gone before his children are grown. People are gathered at the longhouse on the first afternoon, watching and weeping as the "Indian undertakers" gently dress the young man's body in soft, white buckskin. They wrap the dressed body in Pendleton blankets and lift it into the casket, which is draped with more blankets and surrounded with flowers. For the the next two nights, people worship around the the casket—singing, dancing, and praying to exhaustion. New arrivals pay respect by shaking the hand of every person in the longhouse, making a long slow circuit through the crowd. Between sets of Washat songs, impromptu testimony brings the lost friend and family member vividly to mind, and there are open tears. Just before the second dawn breaks, the fatigued mourners have breakfast, setting a portion of the last communal meal by the casket. There is a last song, and to the sound of a single bell, a procession of family and friends follows the casket out to a waiting cattle truck.

184

After an all-night funeral service at the Agency Longhouse, mourners eat breakfast, a small serving of which is set beside the casket in a last sharing of food before the burial ceremony. (Cynthia D. Stowell)

Old people riding in the back of the truck sing plaintively on the long, bumpy journey to the cemetery.

In the gray, early morning light, the casket is lowered with straps into a wooden box inside the grave, head to the west. The box is nailed shut and a tule mat spread on top. As the Farewell Song is chanted, one of the men shovels up some dirt and stands by the grave, while first the men then the women file around the grave, each taking a handful of cold, dry earth and tossing it in the grave. Some people collapse in grief, Shakers with flickering candles lay their healing hands on the suffering, and a quiet chorus of keening and sobbing plays counter-point to the singing. Several men with shovels finish filling the grave, shaping the earth into a smooth mound which is soon covered with flowers, along with the man's trophy belt-buckles, cowboy hat, and other valuables and mementoes. Some mourners go home; others reunite in the longhouse to listen to an elder speaking gently of the young man. "You will not see him again," he tells those who cling to their disbelief, and he shows them pictures and clothing of the young man.

Another meal, and it is time for the widow's giveaway. To pall-bearers, cooks, drummers and singers, she gives new blankets and shawls in appreciation.

Smaller gifts are distributed among the gathered friends. Bedding, dishes, and other household items touched by the man are also given away; some things are kept and bundled up for the memorial dinner and giveaway the next year. The remaining items will be removed from the house and burned. In a few days, the widow is visited by her husband's family, who give her the dark clothing and scarves of mourning, to be worn until the memorial. During that time, she and her children refrain from public activities as much as possible. When her husband's family comes back to her a year later with "clean clothes," or lighter colored clothing, and the memorial dinner and giveaway are held, the widow and her children are "released" and the public mourning period ended. It has all been shared and it feels complete.

Increasingly, shortcuts are taken in these rituals. A family that releases itself after only a month because a powwow is coming up not only receives criticism from the community, but, according to some elders and counselors, is not allowing the grieving process to go its course. The ritual details have roots not in superstition but in basic human needs and the ideal of a balanced natural world. To hurry or alter the rituals is to ignore what the body and the psyche need, to risk throwing off the natural order of things. The tribal mental health programs see many people who have not completed their grieving and have fallen into deep depressions or have adopted self-destructive behaviors. Thus, the cycle of death continues.

The diminished influence of elders on the reservation is in itself an indication of changed values. At one time, elders were the primary sources of wisdom and direction for their people; they were the decision-makers, educators, story-tellers, and disciplinarians, and they occupied a valuable and honored position in the family households. Today the community still speaks of its elders with great respect, their opinions still matter at public meetings and on committees, and they still help to raise grandchildren (often by default). But the old people are likely to live alone in senior citizen housing, outside the mainstream of community life. Instead of their families caring for them, many are looked after by tribal programs which provide pensions, hot meals, firewood, and transportation. Further, it is often not their grandchildren who come to listen to their stories, but researchers from the outside.

As with other reservations, Warm Springs has had its share of non-Indian academics studying its language, history, and culture, often taking their findings back to the universities and leaving nothing behind but informant fees. Now, the Tribes themselves are taking an active role in preserving and re-teaching traditions for future generations. Tribal staff and volunteers have been responsible for recording ceremonies on videotape and film, compiling legends and oral histories, running culture camps for youngsters, developing language dictionaries, teaching native speakers how to teach the language to children and adults, and designing lessons in Sahaptin and Wasco for the tribal newspaper *Spilyay Tymoo* or for KWSO Radio.

The gradual silencing of the native languages on the reservation seems at times like an irreversible cultural loss. Pressured by the boarding school to speak only English, and surrounded as they have been by an English-speaking world, the people of Warm Springs have naturally let their languages go. Vocabularies that were useful in the pre-contact world of fishing, hunting, and gathering have not been systematically updated to include the technology and concepts of twentieth century America. Today, very few people, mostly elders, would consider Sahaptin, Wasco, or Paiute their first language; a few more, mostly the next generation, are bilingual. But the younger generations are usually exposed to the languages only at ceremonies or during school lessons. Efforts to preserve the languages are often met with tribal jealousies or disagreements, gaps in knowledge, or a feeling that the languages should be taught at home. For the most part, they are not spoken at home, and they are slowly dying.

Lately, the Tribes' preservation energies have been focused on the development of a museum to house the wealth of artifacts they are collecting from tribal members. Families are rich with baskets, beadwork, ceremonial clothing, and photographs stored in trunks, out-buildings, and rented storage units. Fire, theft, and

186

financial expediency have made inroads into these valuables, but for the last several years the Tribes have become more aggressive in collecting, cataloguing, and securing privately held artifacts. After many years of planning, they have begun work on the design and concept of the museum itself, which will tell the story of the Warm Springs, Wasco, and Paiute people with displays, dioramas, and live demonstrations.

While the Tribes try to reconstruct and preserve their traditional culture, they are also being urged to respond to the unhappy effects of cultural loss on the people's mental and physical health. It is a loss that many tribal members feel has been accelerated by the Tribes' tendency to focus on economic development. Perhaps it did not occur to the decision-makers that prosperity might actually erode the cultural foundation it was supposed to protect; that it would create competition, isolation, and moral confusion.

The social problems the reservation faces today were in evidence long before the Tribes began their big economic push in the 1950s. In the decades after the people were moved to the reservation, frustrations grew as their culture was discredited, their traditional economy upset, and their political power usurped. This accumulated anger toward the dominant culture is rarely directed at white individuals; instead, the basically peaceable society has turned on itself. Low self-esteem, family violence, poor physical health, accidental injury and death, and suicide have come to plague the reservation. The vehicle that has carried these problems to their present crisis proportions is another of the white culture's offerings—alcohol.

By the Tribes' reckoning, alcohol has been responsible for approximately half the reservation deaths in recent years. During one five-year period (1979–1983), when 124 deaths occurred on the reservation, an alarming one hundred percent of the deaths of people under the age of thirty-six (the median age of death in that period) were alcohol or drug related. Cirrhosis was common with the over-thirty-six group, but accidents, suicides, and homicides accounted for the majority of the alcohol-related deaths in all age groups. According to staff of the Tribal Court and the Youth Services Department, about eighty-five percent

of their 1983 caseload was tied to family or individual alcohol problems.*

These statistics gathered for the Tribes' 1984 "Community Alcohol and Drug Task Force Proposal" were eye-opening confirmation of a community problem that is obvious to anyone who lives in Warm Springs. What has not been as obvious is how to deal with it. Since it affects all segments of the community, from Tribal Council members to teenagers, it has been comfortable either to avoid discussing it out of sheer embarrassment or to encourage camaraderie among drinkers. Only very recently, since the Tribes set alcohol and drug treatment as a reservation priority and launched very visible education and prevention programs, has there been a change in attitude.

Now, with a few prominent community members having opted for treatment, it is much easier for alcoholics to admit they have a problem seek help. The use of off-reservation treatment facilities has also been an attractive alternative for clients.

While the federal government has long recognized and acted on its trust responsibility to provide health care for reservation Indians—beginning with the government physicians promised in the treaties—it has not always defined health problems and solutions in the same way as the reservation population. The Warm Springs Indian Health Center, built by the BIA in the 1930s as a hospital and transferred to the Public Health Service in 1955, has patched up the Warm Springs community for years on an emergency and outpatient basis. In the last decade, it has placed more emphasis on prevention and education, with regularly scheduled pre-natal, well-child, diabetes, otology, and senior citizen clinics. And in 1984, the Indian Health Service (IHS) finally recognized alcohol as a disease by budgeting treatment monies for Warm Springs. But the

---

*Care should be taken when comparing the frequency of alcohol and drug related deaths in Warm Springs with national averages. Generally, the role of alcohol in accidents and violent deaths is not reflected in national figures for lack of documentation; in a small community like Warm Springs, the circumstances of death can be more easily traced, so more data is available.

health center chronically suffers from a small staff and crowded facility as well as the lingering community belief that Indians are "guinea pigs" for inexperienced IHS interns who stay for a year or two and then make their careers elsewhere. Even the presence of a few highly skilled and long-term professionals has not completely counteracted the distrust of government-dispensed health care.

Since the Indian Self-Determination Act of 1975 made it easier for tribes to contract with the federal government for reservation services, the Confederated Tribes have taken more responsibility for defining and providing for their own health needs. An array of community health programs has sprung up over the years, including personal and family counseling, alcohol and drug treatment, foster placement services, group adolescent care, crisis intervention, welfare assistance, employee counseling, and physical fitness. From this diverse collection, the Tribes are trying to fashion a coherent and comprehensive health delivery system that is professional enough to be respected but informal and culturally sensitive enough to be used comfortably.

It has long been believed that traditional Anglo assumptions about health care do not fit with Indian notions about the sources of illness and the paths to wellness. For a time, the best solution seemed to be to employ local caregivers and introduce cultural elements into treatment. The theory was that an Indian, even without training, could empathize with another Indian better than a non-Indian professional, and that through drumming and singing, tanning a hide, or learning the native language, a client would be joined with his culture and made whole again. These tactics have been found to be simplistic and difficult to implement. The Tribes' residential alcohol treatment facility and a wilderness program for adolescents foundered on such assumptions. Professionalism and confidentiality were lacking in many peer treatment efforts.

What the Tribes now seem to be doing is taking what is best in both white and Indian approaches and shaping programs that are both sensitive and successful. Since the alcohol treatment program was disbanded in 1983 and clients have been sent to off-reservation facilities, the rate of successful rehabilitation has soared. At the same time, the Tribes have concentrated more money and staff time on providing professional training for tribal employees. Some Indian para-professionals exposed to modern psychology and medicine have developed a deeper appreciation for Indian "doctoring" because of the ways it parallels and complements modern treatment techniques. Anglo caregivers have become more open to traditional Indian medicine: the IHS will now reimburse traditional Indian healers, and off-reservation hospital staffs have begun to communicate with Indian experts in herbal and spiritual healing to better serve their Indian patients.

Attempts such as these to integrate the offerings of both cultures could well be the key to the survival of the people of Warm Springs as a distinct group. The great success of the Tribes in becoming financially solvent and reasonably independent from the federal government was the first step in ensuring a future for the reservation. Assertion of the Tribes' role as a government lends even more certainty to their survival. But it is their differentness from the dominant culture that perhaps most defines the Tribes as a group. It is what keeps the members from selling off their land and assets and disappearing into the cultural mainstream. It is what isolated them in the first place and is now cherished as their heritage.

When the river tribes first encountered whites, there was a certain openness, a natural mixing of ideas, artifacts, and languages. It is interesting to speculate about what might have happened to Indian people and their cultures had their contact with white people not been interrupted by the reservation system. The cultures might have blended more gently; the natives might have retained their confidence and self-respect and contributed more of their cultural and material strengths to the American fabric, even as their skin lightened and their names changed. But, so too might the Indians have completely disappeared, the victims of irreconcilably different notions about the earth and how to live on it, of the assumption of racial

superiority inherent in "manifest destiny," and of diseases unfamiliar to their bodies. The removal to reservations was a harsh and permanent hiatus in the natural evolution of the Indian people, but it might also have, inadvertently, assisted in their survival.

But survival of what, and at what cost? Isolating the river and basin people on the Warm Springs Reservation and making them dependent on the government resulted in profound cultural shock and defeatism, the effects of which are being felt 130 years after the treaty. Separation of the people from everything familiar to them—their livelihood, their land, their traditions—has set them adrift in a world that is not Indian and not white. But their shared geography, their common history, and their cultural foundation have bound them together as a group with a deep sense of collective identity. It is a fierce sort of pride, fed by adversity and transcending tribal and family differences. In its most positive sense, this "otherness" contains the seed for another flowering of Coyote's people.

It is clearly too late to return to life as it used to be along the Columbia River or in the Great Basin. But the people of Warm Springs have an opportunity like no other since 1855: they remember enough of their traditional culture and are skilled enough in the ways of the white world to be able to choose the best of both and shape their own future. Fairly sure of their survival, they can now consider the quality of their journey into the next century. ☐

BIBLIOGRAPHY

The books, articles and papers listed here, though not all cited in my text, were very helpful to me during the researching and writing of "The Reservation."

American Friends Service Committee. *Uncommon Controversy—Fishing Rights of the Muckleshoot, Puyallup, and Nisqually Indians*. Seattle: University of Washington Press, 1970.

Barnett, H.G. *Indian Shakers—A Messianic Cult of the Pacific Northwest*. Carbondale: Southern Illinois University Press, 1983.

Beckham, Stephen Dow. *The Indians of Western Oregon—This Land Was Theirs*. Coos Bay, Oregon: Arago Books, 1977.

Belloni, Robert C. *United States of America v. State of Oregon*, Civil No. 68–153, Portland, Oregon, April 23, 1969.

Cahn, Edgar S., ed. *Our Brother's Keeper: The Indian in White America*. Washington, D.C.: New Community Press, 1971.

Clemmer, Janice White. "The Confederated Tribes of Warm Springs, Oregon: Nineteenth Century Indian Education History." Ph.D. diss., University of Utah, 1980.

Cliff, Thelma Drake. "A History of the Warm Springs Reservation, 1855–1900." Master's thesis, University of Oregon, 1942.

Confederated Tribes of the Warm Springs Reservation, Annual Reports, 1976–1984.

———. "Briefing Paper, Community Alcohol and Drug Service," February 1986.

———. "Briefing Paper, Indian Health Service Trust Responsibility," February 1986.

———. "Community Alcohol and Drug Task Force Proposal," February 1984.

———. "Comprehensive Plan," 1983.

———. "Constitution and By-Laws," 1938.

———. *Spilyay Tymoo* (Coyote News), 1976–1986.

Cressman, Luther. *Cultural Sequences at The Dalles, Oregon*. Philadelphia: American Philosophical Society, 1960.

Deloria, Jr., Vine and Clifford M. Lytle. *American Indians, American Justice*. Austin: University of Texas Press, 1983.

De Voto, Bernard, ed. *The Journals of Lewis and Clark*. Boston: Houghton Mifflin Co., 1953.

Du Bois, Cora. "The Feather Cult of the Middle Columbia." *General Series in Anthropology*. Menasha: George Banta Publishing Co., 1938.

Fowler, Catherine S. and Liljeblad, Sven. "Northern Paiute." In Warren L. D'Azevedo, ed., *Great Basin*, Vol. 11 of *Handbook of North American Indians*. William C. Sturtevant, general editor. Washington, D.C.: Smithsonian Institution, 1986.

French, David. "Wasco-Wishram." *Perspectives in American Indian Culture Change*. Chicago: University of Chicago Press, 1961.

Gloves, Richard, ed. *David Thompson's Narrative 1784–1812*. Toronto: Champlain Society, 1962.

Hale, Horatio. *Ethnography and Philology* (United States Exploring Expedition, 1838–1942). Ridgewood, N.J: Gregg Press, 1968.

Hunt, Jack. "Land Tenure and Economic Development on the Warm Springs Indian Reservation." *Journal of the West*, 9 (January 1970): 93–109.

Kappler, Charles J., ed. *Indian Affairs, Laws and Treaties*, Vol. II (Treaties). Washington: Government Printing Office, 1904.

Kelly, Isabel T. *Ethnography of the Surprise Valley Paiute*. Berkeley: University of California Press, 1934.

Meacham, A. B. *Wigwam and Warpath*. Boston: John P. Dale and Co., 1875.

Miller, Christopher. *Prophetic Worlds*. New Brunswick, N. J.: Rutgers University Press, 1985.

Mooney, James. "The Ghost Dance Religion and the Sioux Outbreak of 1890." *Fourteenth Annual Report of the Bureau of Ethnology*. Washington, D.C.: Government Printing Office, 1896.

Murdock, George Peter. "Social Organization of the Tenino." *Miscellanea Paul Rivet Octogenario Dictata*, vol. 1. pp. 299–315. Mexico: XXXI Congreso Internacional de Americanistas, Universidad Nacion Autonama de Mexico. (Reprinted in Murdock, *Culture and Society*, 1965).

———. "Tenino Shamanism." *Ethnology*. 4 (1965): 165–171.

———. "The Tenino Indians." *Ethnology*. 19 (1980): 129–149.

Oregon State University. "Warm Springs Research Project," (five volumes). Corvallis, 1960.

Prucha, Francis Paul. *American Indian Policy in the Formative Years*. Lincoln: University of Nebraska Press, 1962.

———. *The Great Father*. Lincoln: University of Nebraska Press, 1984.

———, ed. *The Indian in American History*. New York: Holt, Rinehart and Winston, 1971.

Ramsey, Jarold. *Coyote Was Going There—Indian Literature of the Oregon Country*. Seattle: University of Washington Press, 1977.

Ray, Verne F. *Cultural Relations in the Plateau of Northwestern America*. Los Angeles: Southwest Museum, 1939.

———, et al. "Tribal Distribution in Eastern Oregon and Adjacent Regions." *American Anthropologist*, 40 (1939): 384–415.

Relander, Click. *Drummers and Dreamers*. Caldwell, Idaho: The Caxton Printers, 1956.

Shane, Ralph M. and Leno, Ruby D. *A History of the Warm Springs Indian Reservation, Oregon*. U. S. Department of Interior, Bureau of Indian Affairs, 1949.

Spier, Leslie. *Klamath Ethnography*. Berkeley: University of California Press, 1930.

———. "The Prophet Dance of the Northwest and Its Derivatives: The Source of the Ghost Dance." *General Series in Anthropology*. Menasha: George Banta Publishing, 1935.

Spier, Leslie and Edward Sapir. *Wishram Ethnography*. Seattle: University of Washington Press, 1930.

Steiner, Stan. *The New Indians*. New York: Dell Publishing Co., 1968.

Stewart, Omer C. "The Northern Paiute Bands." *Anthropological Records* 2 (1939): 127–149.

Strong, Emory. *Stone Age on the Columbia River*. Portland: Binfords and Mort, 1959.

Suphan, Robert J. *Oregon Indians II* (Ethnological Report on the Wasco and Tenino Indians). New York: Garland Publishing, 1974.

Trafzer, Clifford E. and Margery Ann Beach. "Smohalla, The Washani, and Religion as a Factor in Northwestern Indian History." *The American Indian Quarterly*. 9 (1985): 309–324.

Washburn, Wilcomb E. *Red Man's Land—White Man's Law*. New York: Charles Scribner's Sons, 1971.

Wheat, Margaret M. *Survival Arts of the Primitive Paiutes*. Reno: University of Nevada Press, 1967.

Wheeler, Erminie Voegelin. "The Northern Paiute of

Central Oregon: A Chapter in Treaty-Making." *Ethnohistory*. 2 (1955): 95–132, 241–72; 3 (1956): 1–10.

Whiting, Beatrice Blyth. *Paiute Sorcery*. New York: Viking Fund Publications in Anthropology, no. 15, 1950.

Wilkes, Charles. *Narrative of the United States Exploring Expedition*. Philadelphia: Lea and Blanchard, 1845.

Zucker, Jeff, Kay Hummel, and Bob Høgfoss. *Oregon Indians: Culture, History and Current Affairs: An Atlas and Introduction*. Portland: Western Imprints, 1983.

INDEX

194

"Altogether it is difficult to leave a country before you have done something to prove that you have felt and loved it."

Vincent Van Gogh ☐
Saint-Rémy, France
1889

COLOPHON

CYNTHIA D. STOWELL is an East Coast native who migrated to the Northwest in 1975 to become acquainted with the region's Indian tribes. During her seven years on the Warm Springs Indian Reservation, Ms. Stowell worked as a tutor, a reporter for the tribal newspaper, and a free-lance writer/photographer. Ms. Stowell, who has a B.A. in sociology from Boston University, currently resides in Portland, Oregon, and works as a writer/photographer. *Faces of a Reservation* is her first book.

Faces of a Reservation uses the typeface Syntax for both text and display. Syntax was designed by the Swiss graphic designer Hans E. Meyer and belongs to a group of typefaces known as Sans Serif Lineales. Typefaces in this group evolved out of an experimental period during the 1920s when many type designers were trying to reduce letter forms to their basic elements.

Photographs were printed as 150-line screen duotones in black and a gray second color (PMS 407). Paper is 70 lb. matte.

The production of *Faces of a Reservation* was accomplished through the professional skills and cooperation of the following:

Typesetting: G&S Typesetters, Inc., Austin, Texas
Printing: Malloy Lithographing, Inc., Ann Arbor, Michigan
Maps: Samuel Gfeller

Faces of a Reservation was designed and produced by the Oregon Historical Society Press.